THE
BETTER BAG
MAKER

An Illustrated Handbook of Handbag Design

Techniques, Tips, and Tricks

Nicole Mallalieu

stashBOOKS.

an imprint of C&T Publishing

Publisher: Amy Marson

Creative Director: Gailen Runge

Art Director / Book Designer: Kristy Zacharias

Editor: S. Michele Fry

Technical Editors: Julie Waldman and Gailen Runge

Production Coordinators: Rue Flaherty and Zinnia Heinzmann

Production Editor: Joanna Burgarino

Illustrator: Mary E. Flynn

Photo Assistant: Mary Peyton Peppo

Cover photography by Nissa Brehmer; **style photography** by Tea Ho, unless otherwise noted; **subject photography** by Diane Pedersen, unless otherwise noted; **how-to photography** by Nicole Mallalieu, unless otherwise noted

Published by Stash Books, an imprint of C&T Publishing, Inc., P.O. Box 1456, Lafayette, CA 94549

Library of Congress Cataloging-in-Publication Data

Mallalieu, Nicole Claire, 1968-

 The better bag maker : an illustrated handbook of handbag design--techniques, tips, and tricks / Nicole Claire Mallalieu.

   pages cm

ISBN 978-1-60705-805-2 (soft cover)

1. Handbags. 2. Sewing. I. Title.

TT667.M345 2014

646.4'8--dc23

                    2013034373

Printed in Malaysia

10 9 8 7

CONTENTS

INTRODUCTION

I'm a self-confessed sewing geek, obsessed with improving my own skills and learning new and better ways of making things. My other passion is sharing that knowledge and watching skills and confidence grow in other people.

I've designed this book to help you become a better bag maker—expanding your repertoire and improving your ability to achieve a professional finish on all your sewing projects. Each project in this book uses the same basic pattern and teaches you a range of techniques for adjusting the proportions of the pattern, as well as constructing pockets, straps, flaps, and bases. Using this variety of techniques, you can transform the basic design into endless different styles. I've merged the skills and tools that I've picked up from working in fashion production, making handcrafted leather goods, dressmaking, quilting, and developing products in the specialized area of handmade fabric bags.

My approach is always "the shortest route to the best finish," and I've included a lot of tips to help you find that path in your own sewing. My tips are often lessons that were hard-won by my own mistakes, or simply by the sheer number of times I've made some parts, always looking for a way to do it faster and better. (My biggest tip, when using this book, is to read the tips!)

You get no reward for doing things the long way with sewing, but you can win praise, appreciation, sales, and awards for making fabulously well-finished fashion accessories. Most important, you can take pride in your own work and enjoy the creative buzz when projects come together quickly.

Through teaching classes in my areas of expertise, I've gained insight into a broad range of learning styles and seen that, given the right pace and clear technique-by-technique instructions, people can improve their skills and confidence and sew better than they ever imagined they could. I've seen the results and I've seen the pride on people's faces. And I believe that I've started more than a few bag-making addictions!

Now it's your turn!

HOW TO USE THIS BOOK

To most effectively learn from this book, start with the first project and become familiar with the basic construction techniques. The projects are ordered by degree of difficulty, each with at least one special technique to gently guide you on to more challenging design features. You can pick and choose your projects or work your way through all of them, as a kind of self-paced bag-making course.

I've graded the skill levels Beginner, Advanced Beginner, Intermediate, and Confident, and some of the bags bridge these levels.

BEGINNER: The beginner projects are designed to introduce the basic concepts of bag making and to increase confidence. You will need to know how to use a sewing machine and understand the basic language of sewing instructions.

ADVANCED BEGINNER: At this stage, confidence is starting to take hold, and you seek new challenges. The projects are designed to introduce minor challenges that have maximum effect and will improve overall skills.

INTERMEDIATE: These projects are designed with the assumption that you have the ability to follow instructions, sew accurately, and understand the sewing machine's capabilities and accessories. The projects are more detailed and will take longer to complete than a basic bag.

CONFIDENT: If you have worked through the other bags in this book, or if you are an experienced crafter who has sewn all sorts of awkward things, then you should feel confident to tackle these more detailed designs. They require the ability to follow more abstract instructions, the strength to manipulate heavily interfaced fabric around a sewing machine, and a solid understanding of your sewing machine. They also require a sturdy sewing machine.

If the instructions look a bit lengthy, it's not because they are complicated, but because they are broken down into tiny steps to guide you through unfamiliar sewing territory. The first time that you make any particular project or bag component will take longer than any other time, and as you repeat the processes, you'll find that you need less guidance and that you've improved both the speed and the quality of your sewing.

You'll notice that many of the techniques are repeated throughout the projects, but each project has another set of techniques to learn. I suggest reading through the instructions first and bookmarking the relevant pages in the Basic Bag-Making Techniques section. As you become increasingly familiar with the basics, you'll spend less time reading these pages (eventually not needing them at all). You can then focus on extending your bag-making repertoire with the new techniques, design ideas, and finishing techniques of the more advanced bag designs.

My method of teaching is to take you slightly beyond your comfort zone, and then to gently guide you to success. If you follow the instructions as you work through each step, I'm sure you'll be amazed at the quality of the work that you can achieve. However, if you'd rather slow down the sense of being "thrown in at the deep end," feel free to substitute any of the more complicated design features with one of the more simple techniques from the Basic Bag-Making Techniques section or another project.

After you've made the projects in this book, you'll have a whole new bag of tricks and design features that can be swapped and changed between projects and also applied to any bag-making project of your choosing. Most likely you will also find that the skills and tips are useful in all sorts of everyday sewing.

Start with small challenges and build up your confidence as you move on through the projects.

Pretty soon, you won't be able to stop making fabulous, fashionable new bags!

TOOLS AND MATERIALS

I've included instructions on the use of specialized interfacings, materials, and gadgets that I use to help make a professionally finished bag come together with minimal fuss. Because of the nature of international trade, some of these products are available worldwide, sometimes with different brand or generic names. Some products may not be available in your part of the world, so it's especially important to understand their properties if you are to substitute with what is available to you.

SEWING MACHINES

If you're in the market for a new machine for bag making, don't be seduced by the number of decorative stitches a machine has. A good motor and strong feeding mechanism are the most essential features. You're better off buying a simple, high-quality machine (even if secondhand) than a less capable machine with bells and whistles that you'll rarely use.

Other handy features are the ability to move needle position, to set the needle to finish in a needle-up or needle-down position, and to change pressure on the presser foot. A knee-operated lift for the presser foot means that you don't have to take your hands away from your work, which gives you greater control over fiddly or unwieldy bag components, and a wide "throat" on the machine (the gap between the needle and the body of the machine) makes it easier to manage large bags and stiff interfacings. (Making bags involves a variety of fiddly, large, stiff, and unwieldy bits!)

NEEDLES

Bag making requires a lot of sewing over bulky seams and dense fabrics, and needle breakages are part of the experience. Always keep a supply of needles of varying size and purpose. When it comes to choosing the right needle, I follow a few general rules of thumb.

- For most bag-related sewing, use regular or universal needles (size 80/12).

- When the going gets tough (and the needles break easily), increase the size of the needle or switch to a needle especially designed for denim (and dense fabrics) or leather. It's always good to have a few of these on hand if you're making bags.

- If you're using fine fabrics for linings, use a fine needle (70/10). A large needle will pucker the fabric or cut holes along the stitch line.

- If your machine is skipping stitches, try changing your needle. It may have become blunt.

PRESSER FEET

Sewing machines usually come with a few standard presser feet, but you may find a few nonstandard feet helpful as well. Read your sewing machine manual to find out what each foot is for, and research what additional feet are available for your machine. If you plan to make a lot of bags and purses, it might be worth investing in a few extras, to make the job easier and the finish better.

As you become increasingly comfortable with your sewing machine and its accessories, you'll get to know which foot to try for which job, and you'll easily switch between them, knowing that the result will be much better with the right foot.

Narrow or Sliding Zipper Foot

A zipper foot that is only on one side of the needle is necessary when stitching into some of the awkward nooks and crannies that you find in bag making. Some machines have a zipper foot that has a wide back section, which extends behind the

needle, and this causes problems when you need to stitch very close to an immovable lump (such as piping cord in a handle or a bag ring in a strap). If this is your machine's standard zipper foot, you may want to invest in a sliding, or adjustable, zipper foot, which will allow you to move the foot to one side or the other of the needle, without any overhanging back section.

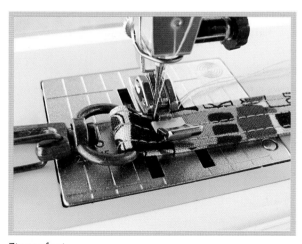

Zipper foot

Walking Foot

Many new machines have a walking foot or dual-feed mechanism as standard. Unlike a standard presser foot, a walking foot or dual feed pushes the top layer of fabric through the machine at the same rate as the feed dogs pull the bottom layer of fabric through. This avoids puckers and twists in bag straps and binding and makes it easier to stitch through bulky fabrics. Not all machines can be fitted with a walking foot, but it might be worth checking the availability of one for your machine.

Walking foot

Denim Foot, Roller Foot, or Height Compensation Tool

Different makes of machine have different solutions for managing very lumpy seams (the sort you get when you're sewing denim or other bulky fabrics). I use a denim foot on my machine. It has a large surface area and a hinged back that allows it to climb over the lumps, instead of getting caught on top. Other machines have roller feet or straight-stitch feet. All of these hold the fabric evenly on the feed dogs and maintain an even stitch on lumpy seams.

Denim foot

If you can't find an equivalent presser foot for your model of machine, other gadgets are available to help you sew over lumps and bumps. When the presser foot is traveling over a lump of fabric, you use one of these tools to fill out the gap underneath the presser foot, and this holds the fabric evenly on the feed dogs beneath.

Some sewing machines have them in their standard toolkit, but if you need to buy one, look for Jean-a-ma-jig, the Hump Jumper, or equivalent products. These tools are often small, flat pieces of plastic, sometimes with a rectangular cutaway section at one end. Others are several small rectangles of plastic held together at one end.

Edge-Stitching Foot

Although it isn't essential, I use this foot all the time. In bag making, you do a lot of edge stitching and stitching in-the-ditch. This presser foot has a guide that travels along the ditch of the seam, and you can set your needle distance evenly from the seam.

Edge-stitching foot

FABRICS FOR BAGS

Almost anything goes for a structured bag like the ones in this book—you'll see that I choose decor-weight or quilting-weight fabrics in most cases. The fabric requirements are based on a 44" width of fabric, although many decor-weight fabrics come in wider widths. I recommend that you don't pick fabrics with a very loose weave, because they will ravel or fray too much and will be difficult to work with.

Prewashing is not necessary, as the bags will rarely be washed. The fabric will look nicer and be easier to work with if it's unwashed.

If your fabric is wide enough, you can cut your straps on the crosswise, but it is best to cut on the lengthwise grain. For best results, do not piece fabrics to create your straps.

INTERFACINGS FOR BAGS

Interfacings are the support materials used between the outer and lining fabrics. When making bags, we usually use fabrics designed for quilting, clothing, or housewares, so we need interfacing to create the appearance and functional stability that a bag requires. Most interfacings in the United States come in a 20" width, and the fabric requirements are based on that number. The exception is fusible fleece, which is typically 40" wide. If your interfacing is a different width, you'll need to add or subtract accordingly from the amounts given.

I use fusible interfacings for bag making because they become a part of the fabric itself, rather than another layer that might sag or move independently. I also strongly believe that it's worth spending money on quality interfacings if you want a quality finish in your bags and purses.

Experiment with interfacings to understand them. Buy small quantities of every interfacing you can find, and fuse them to a range of fabrics to make a labeled swatch set. Test interfacings by themselves, and then test them all again in combination with other interfacings and fusible fleece. It might sound like a lot of messing about, but you'll create

a tactile reference library to use any time you're wondering which interfacing is right for your next bag project. Also consider testing a few interfacing options on the fabric you plan to use on any given bag before you start on the real thing. The more you do this now, the less you'll need to do it in the future.

When I make bags from quilting-weight fabrics, my standard interfacing solution is to fuse a medium-weight, fusible woven cotton interfacing (such as Shape-Flex) securely to the fabric, and then fuse a layer of light fusible fleece to the back of the interfacing. If I want more or less structure than this creates, I tweak the interfacing combination accordingly—using lighter or heavier interfacings or fleece.

Besides the many interfacings that have been developed for the garment industry (which are equally useful for bag making), there are some specialty interfacings that are particularly useful for creating the shapes and structures needed for bag making, and I've recommended them extensively throughout the projects. If you can't find these products, it's worth knowing what they do so that you might be able to find a substitute.

Vilene S320 or Pellon Craft-Fuse

This is nonwoven interfacing that doesn't distort when it is fused. It is lightweight but creates a firm edge that can be used to make a sharp, straight fold line.

It is used extensively as a support when constructing zippered pockets. It is also used in constructing many of the bag components that are sewn with the "turned-edge" technique. That is, the interfacing is fused to the back and used as a base, around which the seam allowances are turned. The components are then stitched together from the right side of fabric.

Vilene S320, which is available in Europe and Australia, has the right sort of structure for this purpose. Pellon Craft-Fuse looks different, but offers similar support. If you can't find these particular products, you will have to experiment with a few interfacings until you find one that doesn't require a lot of heat to fuse, doesn't distort easily, and doesn't stretch.

Pelmet Interfacing (Vilene S520 or Pellon 520F Deco-Fuse)

Pelmet interfacing that is thin, cardboard-like, and fusible is excellent for making structured bag bases. Teamed with template plastic, the effect is absolute stability in the fabric and a flat base in which to insert purse feet. The interfacing also creates a straight edge to define the shape of the bag. If you can't find either of these products, you will have to experiment with the stiffest nonwoven interfacings you can find.

Peltex, Timtex, or fast2fuse

These are stiff, nonwoven interfacings, made from what looks like compressed synthetic fleece. They add the structure of cardboard to fabrics, and so make excellent bag-base materials.

Fast2fuse is thinner than Peltex or Timtex and is fusible on both sides. It comes in medium and heavy. Heavyweight fast2fuse is the best choice for bag bases, and the regular weight is excellent for support in other bag components.

Peltex can be fusible on one side (Peltex 71) or both sides (Peltex 72) and is also available as a sew-in. It's slightly thicker but less dense than fast2fuse and is a good support for bag bases.

Timtex is sew-in (not fusible) but can be used with fusible interfacing to make excellent internal bag bases or be teamed with fusible web (Wonder-Under, Steam-A-Seam, HeatnBond, or the equivalent) if it requires fusing to fabric.

Fusible Fleece

To add loft—or just a bit more substance—you can fuse fleece as well as interfacing to fabric. The reason that both are used is that without the layer of interfacing, the fleece just adds puffiness. The interfacing flattens the fabric and creates a smooth surface, and then the fleece adds loft behind it.

I prefer to use a light synthetic fleece, rather than a quilt batting, simply because I can create fantastic structure without the bulk and weight of batting. Especially with larger bags, the weight of the materials used has to be considered, or the bag will be too heavy.

Different brands and weights of fleece are available. In conjunction with medium-weight inter-facing, high-loft fleece (for example, Vilene H640 and fusible Thermolam Plus) can add stand-up structure to a bag and is easier to sew than some of the more rigid interfacings that give a similar look. Low-loft fleece (such as Vilene H630), when fused to the back of interfacing, gives soft structure and body. Pellon 987F is a dense, felt-like fleece, which gives support and structure that sits somewhere between the two weights of Vilene fleece. Fusible Warm Fleece 1 is slightly lighter than Pellon 987F.

Clever use of interfacing and fleece combinations will allow you to mix and match different weights of fabric on the same bag and give them all the same structural properties. For example, stiffer interfacing or bulkier fleece on a light fabric can help make the light fabric hold the same shape as a heavier fabric with a lighter combination of interfacing and fleece.

When adding fleece to fabric, you must always be aware of the bulk that can build up on converging seams and take care to reduce or remove fleece from seam allowances wherever possible.

QUICK GUIDE TO INTERFACINGS

Fusible Nonwoven Interfacing		
Light to medium, stable	Vilene S320 Pellon Craft-Fuse Bosal Shirt Fuse	Bosal Dura-Fuse Pellon 950F ShirTailor
Heavy (pelmet)	Vilene S520	Pellon 520F Deco-Fuse
Stiff	fast2fuse HEAVY Peltex 71, Peltex 72	Timtex (not fusible) Bosal CRAF-TEX
Fusible Woven Interfacing		
Light	Any brand fusible gauze-weight woven fabric base	
Medium–light	Bosal Fashion-Fuse Pellon Shape-Flex	HTC Form-Flex
Fusible Fleece		
Light	Vilene H630	Fusible Warm Fleece 1
Medium	Bosal Fusible Batting Pellon 987F	Vilene H640 HTC Fusible Fleece
Webbing Products		
	Wonder-Under Steam-A-Seam HeatnBond Vliesofix	Splendid Web Applifix Mistyfuse

Other Support Materials

A few other support materials can be used to hold the shape of straps and bases on fabric bags: piping cord, plastic tubing, polyester boning (such as Rigilene), and template plastic. These can all be purchased from general sewing and craft-supply stores.

PIPING CORD

Piping cord is soft cotton cord that is mostly used to make piping for home furnishings but equally useful in bag making. As well as being the support for piping, it can be used for plumping up bag straps to make them more comfortable to carry.

TIP:

To stop piping cord from unraveling, wrap it with sticky tape before cutting.

PLASTIC TUBING

Flexible plastic tubing can serve the same purpose as piping cord, but unlike piping cord, it holds its shape in a smooth, springy curve.

POLYESTER BONING

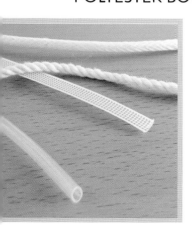

Boning is made from thin polyester rods that are woven into a flat, ribbon-like material so that it can be stitched with a sewing machine. It's mostly used in dressmaking, costuming, and corsetry to hold rigid lines and curves. In bag making, it can be used for internal supports as well as in straps.

TEMPLATE (STENCIL) PLASTIC

Template, or stencil, plastic is a flexible, springy sheet of semitransparent plastic used in patchwork to make templates of pattern pieces. It also provides lightweight, durable support for flat bag bases, particularly when purse feet are added. The plastic is sturdy enough to hold a flat shape, yet flexible enough to stitch through on a normal domestic sewing machine and manipulate when you turn a bag through to the right side.

ADHESIVES

I have a background in both fabric and leather bag making and tend to merge the techniques for both disciplines, even when I'm working with fabric alone.

When you work with leather, there are no pins, and you can't get away with unpicking mistakes, so pieces are glued or taped together before sewing. I use this technique with fabric whenever it's a shortcut to a better finish, which is frequently. Instead of pins holding fabric pieces together, I simply fuse or glue the fabric into place and then stitch over the top. It greatly reduces the stress and chance of error.

Fusible Webbing

Fusible webbing (such as Wonder-Under, Vliesofix, Steam-A-Seam, or HeatnBond) is like a film of plastic fibers on parchment paper. It creates a bond when it's fused between layers of fabric, and the backing paper allows you to cut, place, and fuse it accurately, one side at a time. It's a very controllable, strong adhesive and works brilliantly to hold fabrics together before stitching. It is extremely useful when constructing fancy straps and fiddly details on bags, because there is no need to pin and hold the fabrics as you sew.

The backing paper on fusible webbing is as useful as the webbing part, as it creates a sharp folding edge for seam allowances and turnings. Iron-on hem tape (with no paper) can be used as a substitute for fusible webbing when the backing paper is not needed as an edge for folding fabric.

Fusible Tape

Throughout my instructions, I refer to fusible tape, and by this, I mean rolls of narrow-cut fusible webbing, made by manufacturers such as Vliesofix, Steam-A-Seam, Wonder-Under, and HeatnBond.

I use ¼″ fusible tape because it's a convenient width for holding zippers and patch pockets in place, and it's what I'm used to handling. Like fusible webbing, the paper backing on fusible tape is useful as a sharp folding edge for fabric and turnings.

When I occasionally run out of fusible tape, I cut fusible webbing into narrow strips with a rotary cutter and ruler.

Quilt-Basting Spray

Quilt-basting spray is aerosol spray glue that holds fabrics together long enough to stitch things in place. I absolutely love it because its hold is strong but repositionable, and its application is superfast. I use it in almost every bag project I make to hold straps, fabric overlay details, and other bag components together as I sew. Because of the broad area covered by the spray, it isn't suitable for fine detail work. (I use fabric gluestick or fusible tape for fine work.) You want a spray with a firm hold, that won't gum up your sewing machine needle.

TIP:

Place the bag components in the bottom of a cardboard box when you need to spray them. This contains the spray. I call this my "spray booth."

Fabric Glues

Take the time to investigate the gluesticks and adhesives available at your local fabric store or craft show. New glue pens and sticks are coming onto the market all the time.

I'm a huge fan of my gluestick pens because they can be used to hold down the smallest, fiddliest corners and turnings; they give more control than pins; and they often take the place of basting or stay stitching, making the whole process of sewing bags faster and more effective.

Gluestick

TIP:

When using fusible materials, you'll need to protect both your ironing board and iron; a Teflon appliqué mat will serve this purpose for a lifetime. Baking parchment is a functional substitute, but over time it will cost you far more than a mat.

HAND TOOLS

Tailor's Awl / Stiletto

A tailor's awl is a spike with a small handle. It is used as a kind of movable pin (or long, pointy finger) to hold awkward things in place as you sew them by machine. It's also useful for transferring dot-placement marks from pattern to fabric and for pulling out turned-through corners on bag flaps and straps. It's an inexpensive and worthwhile tool, and I'd be lost without mine. (I have about six of them!)

Hera Marker

A Hera marker subtly creases or dents the fabric so that you can see where to stitch or place a pocket or other add-on detail. Hera markers can be a rotary or solid style, but the main feature is an edge that is sharp enough to mark without damaging the fabric.

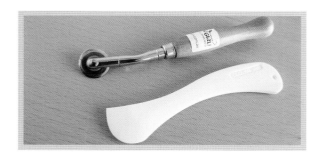

Seam Ripper

You may not think that there is much difference between seam rippers until you use a quality one, with a fine point and sharp blade. No matter what level of sewing experience we have, we all make mistakes and need to unpick. The sharper and finer the seam ripper, the less time you'll spend unpicking. It's as simple as that.

Saddler's Punch

A $^3/_{16}$"- or $^1/_4$"-diameter hole punch that can be hammered hard through several layers of fabric, leather, or plastic is much easier to use than any plier-style punch tool. Saddlery suppliers and some hardware stores sell these as single tools or in sets with multiple sizes.

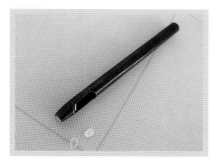

Saddler's punch

FABRIC MARKERS

In recent years, there have been a lot of developments in the area of fabric markers. Along with the usual range of chalks and quilter's or dressmaker's pencils, a huge range of water-soluble, heat-soluble, and air-soluble disappearing-ink marker pens are now available—as are duo sets of marker and marker-remover pens. These allow you to draw on fabric to mark placements and stitch lines, and the ink disappears when it is exposed to the appropriate solvent (air, water, heat, or chemicals). Also fine-point refillable fabric-marker pencils come in several colors, which allow you to mark clear, accurate placement lines on the fabric. They usually have an eraser as well.

Of course, the old-fashioned methods of tailor's tacking and pinning still work, but being able to draw clear lines on the right side of the fabric helps you to stitch straight lines and place design features squarely where they ought to be.

PRESSING EQUIPMENT

Pressing seams as you sew is an important part of making a well-finished bag. A good final press will make the most of all the care you've put in to the making. It's like a final polish. I have almost as many tools for pressing as I do for cutting, marking, and sewing, and I use all of them all the time.

Iron

A good steam iron is an essential tool in the sewing room. You need one that can hold high heat and produce a good surge of steam.

Ironing Press

An ironing press makes the business of fusing interfacing fast and efficient, and if you plan to make a lot of bags, it will get a lot of use. Although a new press can be several hundred dollars, a secondhand press will cost much less.

Ironing Boards

If you can find a sleeve pressing board (like a miniature ironing board), in addition to a standard ironing board, it is a worthwhile investment. A bag becomes increasingly awkward to press as it nears completion, and a small, narrow ironing board supports side seams and other isolated areas so that you can press them without affecting other areas of the bag.

Wooden Things

Lengths of dowel and quad (wood molding that looks like a quarter cylinder) make excellent pressing (and turning) tools for bag straps. Wooden spoons, curtain rods, and broom handles may substitute, but beware of varnish or oils in the wood that may mark your fabric.

Fabric Supports

Pressing hams and sleeve rolls can be purchased from fabric stores and can be somewhat useful, but I prefer to use dense fabric cloths, such as pure cotton moleskin or well-washed denim or canvas. These can be folded or rolled into any shape, or held flat to the inside of a bag to support awkward corners and places that can't be managed around an ironing board.

Pressing Cloth

A pressing cloth, whether a simple piece of cotton lawn or a chemically treated cloth (such as a Rajah Pressing Cloth), is necessary when fusing synthetic interfacings and fleece to fabric. You sometimes also need to protect the right side of your fabric from the scorch or shine of an iron, and I'd recommend a Rajah cloth for this.

CUTTING EQUIPMENT

In addition to sharp scissors for cutting fabric, consider:

Rotary Cutters

Used with a quilting ruler and a cutting mat, a rotary cutter can quickly cut straight, accurately measured lines. I recommend that you use all three for all the projects in this book (which are all based on rectangles). Together, they increase accuracy and keep all the lines straight and square, which makes it easier to achieve a very sharply defined, professional finish.

Point Cutters

Olfa makes a rotary point cutter with a rounded blade and a point at the top so it can roll inward to nick a notch mark or cut into a corner point. It can also cut back from an accurately placed point so that you don't snip into stitches.

Appliqué Scissors

These are known as *duckbill* scissors in some parts of the world, because of the flat, semicircular shape of one of the blades. This blade is designed to hold backing fabric out of the way as the points of the scissors snip away excess fabric at the front. They are useful in reducing the bulk of interfacings and seam allowances on converging bag seams.

Pinking Shears

Pinking shears cut a zigzag line that serves two purposes: reducing bulk in curved seam allowances quickly and stopping raw edges of fabric from fraying.

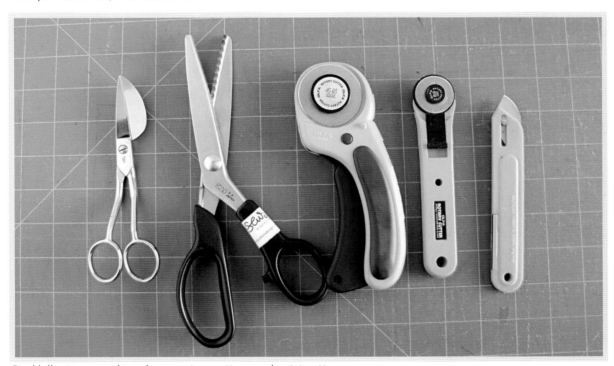

Duckbill scissors, pinking shears, rotary cutters, and point cutter

KEY SKILLS

Now that you have the basic tools to make professional-looking bags, we'll look at the key skills that are used at any level—from beginner to advanced—and repeated throughout the projects.

At first, you may have to flip between the sections of this book to complete a project. After you have used these core skills a few times, you won't need this section as much, and you can focus on learning new (and increasingly advanced) techniques in each project.

INTERFACING

How to Choose Interfacing

Before you cut and prepare the fabric and interfacing for a project, test the interfacing on fabric (page 10). Also test the heat setting required to fuse the interfacing securely without scorching or shrinking it. Many manufacturers have this sort of information on their websites, but sometimes when you purchase interfacing, you don't actually have access to the manufacturer's name or the product name, so it's good to be able to work this out for yourself.

You need a few sacrificial scraps of the interfacing and fabric and a few rules of thumb. The rest is experimentation and taking notes.

The rules of thumb that I use are:

- Synthetic fibers melt when too much heat is applied. Always use a pressing cloth between the back of the interfacing and the iron. Even if the iron is not too hot, residue from the interfacing can build up on the surface of the iron.

- Lightweight interfacings shrink and bubble with too much heat. When fusing lightweight interfacing, err on the side of too cool rather than too hot an iron. If the interfacing doesn't stick after pressing down with the iron for 5 seconds, increase the heat a little. Work out the optimal heat setting by increasing the heat until the interfacing actually does bubble and shrink. Take note of the optimal setting.

- Medium- and heavyweight cotton interfacings need higher heat and pressure than synthetics and lightweight interfacings, and you won't need a pressing cloth. Increase the heat on the iron, and press down hard for 5–10 seconds. If the interfacing doesn't fuse to the fabric, press harder and for longer. If that doesn't work, increase the heat again.

An ironing press will make using these interfacings a breeze, because it can hold high heat and pressure over a larger area than a domestic iron can.

- Make sure that the interfacing is completely fused to the fabric before adding another layer of interfacing or fleece to the back of it. Fleece and other interfacings might require a completely different heat and pressure setting than the interfacing on the fabric, and in trying to set one, you may shrink or burn the other. *Never attempt to fuse more than one layer at a time.*

- Fusible fleece needs steam and very little pressure to bond it to fabric. Place it adhesive side down on the back of the interfaced fabric, and use a damp pressing cloth and dry iron (or a steam iron and dry pressing cloth) to gently fuse it in place.

How to Fuse Interfacing

1. Before you fuse interfacing to fabric, press the fabric very well. If you're using cotton or linen, use a lot of heat and steam to ensure that it's very flat and smooth and that any shrinkage in the fabric happens before the interfacing is applied.

2. Fusible interfacing has an adhesive that is set by heat, which bonds it to the fabric. When you pick up a piece of interfacing, check which side has the adhesive. The adhesive side is often slightly shiny or a little rougher to touch than the nonstick side. The adhesive side goes to the wrong side (back) of the fabric.

3. With the iron on the appropriate heat setting (of course, you've tested it and know this) and a pressing cloth over the interfacing if necessary, press downward onto the interfacing until it fuses to the fabric. Gently glide the iron (without pressure) to the next unfused area, and then press down again onto the interfacing. Keep doing this until the whole piece is fused to the fabric. An ironing press makes this job much faster.

Block Fusing

I prefer to block fuse interfacing before cutting out bag pieces. This means fusing interfacing to the fabric before cutting. It avoids the distortion that can happen to individually cut and fused fabric and interfacing and increases accuracy.

When you are instructed to block fuse and cut a bag piece, simply place the required pattern piece on the interfacing, and roughly (quickly and without measuring) cut about ½" to ¾" larger around the pattern piece. Fuse the rough-cut interfacing to the fabric, and then (using the pattern) accurately cut out the required bag pieces.

When it's necessary to cut interfacing without seam allowances, fuse the interfacing (cut accurately without seam allowances) to the uncut fabric, and then use the pattern or a quilting ruler and rotary cutter to add seam allowances as you cut the fabric to the pattern shape.

REDUCING BULK

When you add interfacing to fabric to create structure where you need it, you're often also adding it to areas that don't need it.

In some parts of a bag, interfacing in the seam allowances adds support and creates shape; in other areas it becomes problematic, especially where seams converge. Interfacing on seam allowances can contribute to the kind of bulk that a sewing machine will refuse to sew. Needles may break, and frustration will follow!

Cutting without Seam Allowances on the Interfacing

You'll see instructions throughout the projects for cutting interfacing shorter than strap ends and sometimes cutting interfacing without seam allowances.

To cut a square or rectangle piece without seam allowances, cut the interfacing to the pattern shape, and then use a quilting ruler and rotary cutter to slice 1" off the width and 1" off the height of the cut piece. (This instruction only applies if the seam allowance is ½"—if you have a different seam allowance, you will need to trim the interfacing accordingly.)

Removing Interfacing from Seam Allowances

When the interfacing is block fused to the fabric, it is trimmed away from problem areas after the seams are sewn. This allows you to reduce the bulk back to the actual stitch line, which makes it easy to press the seam allowances flat and open.

You may find trimming interfacing from seam allowances time-consuming and tedious. I think the time saved by avoiding inaccurate cutting makes up for the time spent removing interfacing, and the finished effect makes it completely rewarding.

I keep devising new, faster ways of removing interfacing from seam allowances. Here are a few methods:

- Duckbill or appliqué scissors help you to separate the interfacing from the fabric as you carefully snip it away. Slow and steady.

- On heavier fabrics, if you use woven interfacing (cut on the straight grain), you can often just tear it off the seam allowances in one neat strip. This is much faster than cutting.

- Carefully use a sharp seam ripper to slice through the interfacing and fleece along the outer edge of a seam, and then peel it off the seam allowance of the fabric. This takes practice and care and only works with the very sharpest of seam rippers, but it is very fast and effective.

Pressing

Pressing the seams open all the way to the end of the seam is important to ensure that the bulk is evenly distributed when seams converge.

The Corner Rule

I have a technique that in Australia I call "the 3cm rule." To work in inches, we could say "the scant 1¼" rule," but it might be a bit wordy, so let's just call it "the corner rule." The rule is that on ½" seam allowances, snip from the very end of the seamline to about 1³⁄₁₆" down the edge of the seam allowance—this will create the optimum angle to reduce bulk and yet allow you to press the seam allowances open right to the end of the seam.

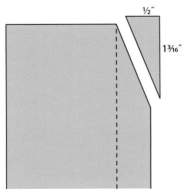

With different width seam allowances, the length of the clipping changes— it's always just a little over twice the depth of the seam allowance—but the angle that you create remains the same. Throughout the projects, I've recommended different lengths to clip away, but with practice, you'll develop an eye to instinctively see what needs to be clipped to create the correct angle.

STARTING AND STOPPING AND KEEPING ENDS NEAT

Bag making involves a lot of highly visible stitching. Here are a few tricks to make ends neat.

Hold the Threads

Sometimes the feed dogs can be a little slow to grip the fabric and move it through the machine. In the meantime, the upper thread and bobbin thread can tangle on the underside of the fabric. This can be remedied by winding both the upper and bobbin threads around your finger until the stitches form correctly.

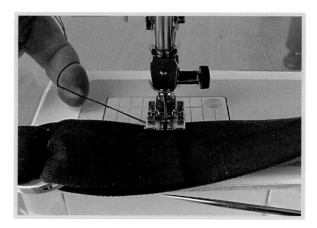

1. As you begin to sew, pull on the threads with your finger as you guide the fabric through the first few stitches. The threads will feel loose for a few stitches, and then you'll feel them "bite" the fabric.

2. After the threads are locked into the stitches, reverse a few stitches (backstitch) while still holding the threads, and then stitch forward again, over the backstitching.

3. After a few stitches (when the fabric is moving easily through the machine), you can let go of the threads and continue to sew normally.

Pull the Threads to the Back

If you want to eliminate thread ends or the chance that they might unravel, you can pull them out of sight and glue, tie, or thread them out of the way. This isn't always necessary, but it is a fine finishing technique that can make a difference on highly visible top-stitching details.

1. At the end of a row of top stitching, take extra care to backstitch (reversing no more than 4 stitches and then stitching forward no more than 3) neatly over the existing stitches.

2. If the underside of the top stitching is visible on the finished project, cut the threads with at least 3″ length. If the underside is not going to be visible, you can cut the threads as short as ¾″.

3. From the underside of the fabric, pull the bobbin thread until the upper thread appears as a loop. Use your fingernails, an awl, pin, or seam ripper to pull the loop through to the underside of the fabric.

4. If the underside of the fabric is not going to be visible on the finished project, you can leave the threads long, or trim them to ½" and fuse a strip of webbing over the top of them. They won't unravel.

If the underside of the fabric will be visible (for example, on a strap), tie the threads together as close to the fabric as possible; then trim off the excess thread.

To completely hide the thread ends (instead of trimming), thread them through a needle and stitch them into the fabric, pulling the needle through a long stitch between the layers of fabric. Pull the thread a little tight and then trim off the excess thread so that the end disappears under the surface of the fabric.

STITCHING SHARP EDGES AND SMOOTH CURVES

Stitching close to a folded edge or seam, from the right side of fabric, holds layers of fabric together so that they move in a single, smooth line, accentuating a curve or sharpening a straight line.

Interfacing on the seam allowances can add structural support to curves and sharp edges (although it needs to be removed from areas where seams meet). Three main types of stitching are used for this purpose: top stitching, edge stitching, and under stitching.

Top Stitching

Top stitching is always sewn with the right side of fabric uppermost on the machine. It can be decorative, but in most cases it also serves a structural purpose.

Top stitching can be used to attach details like patch pockets or tabs on zippers, hold straps flat, and accentuate design lines. By topstitching around the top of a bag or on vertical seamlines, edges are defined and the bag stays upright. Topstitch around a flap or strap, and the fabric curves smoothly around the bag's shape.

If you topstitch ¼″ from the edge of a seam (for example, around a flap or the top of the bag), the seam will sit in a smoother line than if it's left without top stitching. If you want to make a seamed edge look even smoother and flatter, stitch 2 rows—the first one ¹⁄₁₆″ from the seam and the second row ¼″ from the first—catching all of the seam allowances to the wrong side (or inside) of the bag. If there is interfacing on the seam allowance, top stitching can make it behave as a structural support to hold the shape of the seamed edge.

Matching thread color to fabric color is important when topstitching. Unless you know that you can be very neat, don't use a contrast thread because every inaccuracy will be plainly visible. If the fabric has mostly one color, use that color thread. If the fabric has a range of colors or tones, use one of the midtones, which will be less visible. If you're using different fabrics on a bag, change the thread as often as needed to match the fabric that you're sewing.

Edge Stitching

Edge stitching is another name for top stitching that is between ¹⁄₁₆″ to ⅛″ from a seamline. It defines a seamline with both the decorative effect of the stitches and the smoothing effect of holding seam allowances firmly to the underside of the fabric.

Edge stitching can be used on both sides of the seam, with seam allowances pressed open (and caught underneath by the stitches), or on one side of the seam, with all seam allowances turned to that side.

Under Stitching

Under stitching is a form of edge stitching, but it is always on a facing or lining side of a seamed edge. Understitching ¹⁄₁₆″ from the seam holds the seam allowances to the inside fabric and allows the outer fabric to fold over the crisp line that is created. It defines the top edge of a bag and creates smooth curves on seamed edges.

HOW TO UNDERSTITCH THE TOP EDGE OF A BAG

1. Sew the facing to the top edge of the bag with a ½″ seam allowance.

2. Turn the fabric to the right side (so that you can see the right side of the seam). On the underside, fold the seam allowances toward the facing side of the seam.

3. Using 3 fingers on each hand to gently open and flatten the right side of the seam, and with your thumb underneath (keeping the seam allowances in position), topstitch ¹⁄₁₆″ from the seam, around the facing.

4. If the top edge of the bag is curved, trim the seam allowances to ⅛″ from the under-stitching stitches. If the edge of the bag is straight, you don't need to trim the seam allowances.

5. Fold the facing to the inside of the bag, using the firm line that the under stitching creates to push the seam to the very top of the bag. Press from both the outside and facing sides to make the edge as flat as possible.

6. On the right side of the outer bag, topstitch ¼″ from the top edge of the bag, all the way around the bag.

7. Marvel at the lovely smooth line that you've just created on your bag.

BASIC BAG-MAKING TECHNIQUES

These are the techniques used for the projects in this book, and indeed for many other bag-making projects. You can use this section as a stand-alone reference for any bag making that you do.

In each of the projects, I refer to this section when you need to make straps, a base, or pockets. As you work through the book, you will probably consult this section less and less. You may also gain the confidence to swap techniques around and start making up your own variations on my designs.

ALTERING PATTERNS

The projects in this book are all based on the same basic rectangular structure, but a few simple pattern alterations can make them look radically different.

Before you alter any pattern, it's a good idea to sew together a sample made from the original pattern. For the purposes of this book, that means making the basic bag straight from the pattern (pullout pages P1–P4). This way, you'll learn which pattern pieces make each part of the bag and will easily be able to visualize where and how the alterations work on each pattern piece.

The techniques of *slash and open* and *slash and close* allow you to change the width and length of bag components while maintaining the positions of key pattern markings. Once you understand these basic techniques, you'll be free to customize any bag pattern in the same way.

The pattern pieces all have slash lines marked on them, and the individual project instructions will direct you to add to or subtract from the pattern length or width at these lines. When you trace off a new pattern alteration, label each pattern piece with exactly what the alteration is and file it. Some of the projects will use the same alterations as others, and some pieces will be interchangeable, so it's worth keeping the whole collection.

Slash and Open

When you want to make a bag wider or longer than the original pattern, you will *slash* the pattern and add in extra width or length. You could physically slash (cut) the pattern, add in extra paper, and tape it together, but tracing gives more accurate results and will preserve the original pattern.

1. Take a piece of paper that is larger than the pattern piece and trace all of the slash lines on the original pattern—vertical and horizontal—to create a framework on which to build the new pattern. They will help you to keep the 2 halves of the pattern aligned and square when you make the alteration.

2. Decide where the extra width or length needs to be added in the pattern, and identify the slash line that will be used. (For the projects in this book, you'll be given this instruction).

3. Trace the first part of the pattern, including all notches and pattern markings, to the slash line that will be used. (Fig. A)

4. Measure the required extra length or width away from the slash line, and draw a parallel line at this distance. (Fig. B)

5. Align the new line with the slash line on the original pattern, and check that the horizontal slash lines on the pattern line up with the horizontal lines that you traced in Step 1. When it's all square and accurately aligned, trace the second part of the pattern. Remember to trace the notches and pattern markings, *except* center-front/center-back (CF/CB) if your slash has affected this area. (Fig. C)

6. Join the lines of the pattern pieces and, if necessary, mark in a new CF/CB notch in the center of the expanded section or sections. (Fig. D)

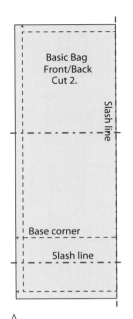

A.

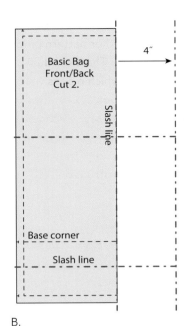

B.

C.

D.

7. Repeat the process, adding exactly the same measurement at the corresponding slash lines on any other pattern piece that has to match to this piece. The individual project instructions will tell you which pieces will need to be altered, but if you look at a finished bag sample, you should be able to see which pattern pieces will be affected by changing the dimensions of one piece. If you get used to thinking it through this way, you'll need less instruction.

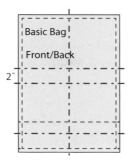

NOTE:

There are 2 slash lines called "horizontal slash line #2" on the bag base and bag base support pattern pieces and 2 slash lines called "vertical slash line #2" on the side panel and lining side panel pieces. These correspond with the slash lines on the facing piece, and if you expand or reduce the same measurement at each of these lines, the pattern will match together perfectly.

Slash and Close

This is a similar process to slash and open, but instead of adding extra width or length, you're reducing it.

1. Identify the slash line where the pattern reduction will be made. (In the projects in this book, you'll be given this instruction).

2. Above or below this line (whichever side interferes with the fewest pattern markings), measure out the width or length that you need to reduce, and draw a line parallel to the slash line at this measurement. Essentially, you will be cutting out the section between the 2 lines.

3. Trace the first part of the pattern, including any pattern markings, from an edge to the original slash line. Also trace any transecting slash lines, which will help to keep the pattern aligned as you trace the next part.

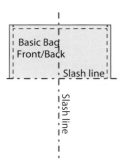

4. Align the slash line of the pattern piece you've just traced with the new slash line on the original pattern (see Step 2). Check that the transecting lines on the original and new patterns are aligned, and trace the next part of the pattern.

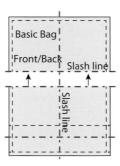

5. Label all the pattern pieces with the adjustment that you've made, and file them carefully.

TECHNIQUES

BASIC POCKETS

Patch Pocket

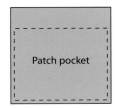

Patch pocket

DOUBLE-TURN THE TOP EDGE

1. Cut the pocket piece in the lining fabric of your choice, using the patch pocket pattern piece #22 (or any other square or rectangular pocket shape).

2. Across the top edge, fold 1¾" toward the wrong side of fabric and press a crease along the fold line. Turn under ¾" and press another crease. (If you prefer, you can fold the ¾" turning first, followed by the 1" turning).

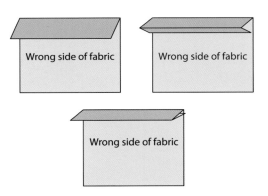

Wrong side of fabric

Wrong side of fabric

Wrong side of fabric

3. Unfold the turnings and clip the corners of the top edge from each end of the top crease to 1½" along the top edge. Fold and press the turnings back into place.

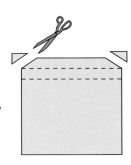

4. Topstitch the turning to the pocket piece, ⅙" from the edge of the bottom folded edge.

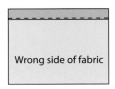

Wrong side of fabric

PRESS THE TURNINGS

1. On the wrong side of the fabric, press generous ¼" turnings, pressing the bottom edge first, followed by the 2 side edges.

TIP:

This is a lot easier if you fuse ¼" of fusible tape around the 3 raw edges of the pocket, on the wrong side of fabric, and use the backing paper as an edge to fold against.

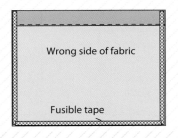

Wrong side of fabric

Fusible tape

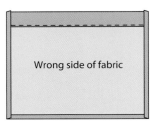

Wrong side of fabric

2. Unfold the bottom corners of the turnings, and clip the corners of the bottom turning from the end of the fold line to ½" down the raw edge of fabric. Peel the backing paper off the bottom turning, and press the clipped turning into place.

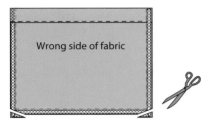

3. At both the top and bottom corners of the side turnings, fold and press the tips of the turnings in toward the fold line, at a 45° angle from the fold line. This will help to hide the raw edges of fabric when the pocket is being sewn to the lining.

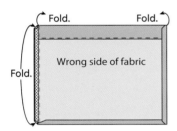

4. Removing all the backing paper from fusible tape, fold and press the side turnings into place.

ATTACH THE POCKET TO THE LINING

1. Center the pocket piece, right side up on the right side of fabric, on one of the bag lining pieces.

2. Pin, fuse, or glue the side and bottom edges of the pocket to the lining.

3. Beginning at the top-right-hand side of the pocket, stitch as close to the edge as you can, around to the upper-left-hand corner. Pivot and stitch a ¼" U-turn, and then stitch a second row, ¼" in from the first, all the way back to the top-right-hand corner.

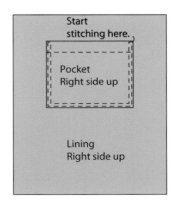

Compartment Pocket

NOTE:

If the pattern for your project has been slashed and opened or closed along vertical slash line #1, then alter this pattern piece in the same way. If the pattern for your project has been slashed and closed on horizontal slash line #1, check that the finished compartment pocket will fit between the base corner notch and (at minimum) ¾" from the top edge of the lining piece. Any excess can simply be trimmed off the bottom of the pocket piece.

1. Cut the compartment pocket (pattern piece #8) in the lining fabric.

2. Along the long top edge of the compartment pocket piece, fold and press a ½" turning toward the wrong side of fabric. Turn and press the fabric again, making the second turning level with the notches at the side edges.

3. While you're still at the ironing board, turn and press a generous ¼" turning toward the wrong side of fabric along the bottom edge of the pocket piece.

TIP:

If you fuse ¼" fusible tape to the right side of fabric along the bottom edge of the pocket, the backing paper will stabilize it so you can easily fold an even ¼" turning. Then when you're ready to attach the pocket to the lining fabric, you can remove the backing paper and fuse the pocket into place. No need for pins!

4. At the top of the pocket piece, stitch the double-turning to the pocket fabric, a scant ¹⁄₁₆" from the folded bottom edge of the turning. You may stitch along the top folded edge also if you want.

5. Fold and press creases to mark pocket divisions. You need to divide the pocket into at least 2 compartments (or the pocket will gape open), but you can divide it into 3 or more. If you want to carry narrow tools or pens, you can make pockets to fit them.

6. Place the compartment pocket (right side up) on the right side of the lining piece, aligning the top edge of the pocket with the notches on the side seams of the lining (or follow the directions in the individual patterns for shallower bags). Pin, fuse, or glue the side seams and bottom edge of the pocket to the lining.

7. Topstitch the bottom edge of the compartment pocket to the lining, ⅟₁₆″ from the folded edge.

NOTE:

If you have an exposed or basic zipper pocket on the lining that is under this pocket, take care not to stitch through the pocket bag/ lining.

8. If you haven't fused or glued the side seam edges together, stitch the pocket to the lining ¼″ in from the side seam edges.

9. Use a Hera or fabric marker to draw a line ¼″ in from the bottom row of stitches. Also draw a parallel line ¼″ from each of the pocket division lines (creases).

10. Topstitch along the line (¼″ in from the top stitching) at the bottom edge of the pocket, but when you reach a pocket division line, pivot and stitch toward the top of the pocket. At the top edge of the pocket, stitch a small U-turn and then stitch a parallel row, following the line ¼″ from the first, back down to the horizontal line. Pivot and continue to topstitch the bottom edge of the pocket and any other pocket divisions in the same manner.

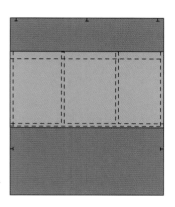

11. Press the pocket flat.

ZIPPERED POCKETS

Basic Zippered Pocket

With this basic pocket technique, you can make internal zippered pockets (between the lining and the outer bag) that are safe and discreet. You can change the length of the zipper pocket to fit any zipper length, simply by changing the length of the facing and width of the pocket piece.

TIP:

If you are making a pocket to fit a particular zipper, remember to measure the zipper at least ⅛″ longer on each end, so that you won't hit the metal stoppers as you topstitch around the pocket opening. Alternatively, if you want to use a zipper that is longer than the pocket, you may shorten the zipper (page 39).

CUT AND PREPARE THE POCKET PIECES

1. Cut the basic bag pocket (pattern piece #23) in lining fabric. Some projects will require you to shorten the length of this piece.

2. Cut the zipper pocket 1 facing (pattern piece #9) in lining fabric and also in interfacing (Vilene S320 or Pellon Craft-Fuse are excellent for this), but do not fuse them together yet.

NOTE:

If you can't find an interfacing that doesn't distort when it's fused, use a very light interfacing and skip Step 3. Instead, fuse the interfacing to the wrong side of the pocket facing piece and then draw the stitch line on the interfacing, using a ruler and pencil.

3. Use a sharp pencil (or marker) and ruler to trace the stitch line from the pattern piece onto the non-fusible side of the interfacing. Using a rotary cutter and ruler, cut along the stitch line on the interfacing, removing that section of the interfacing completely.

NOTE:

It's important to cut the interfacing as straight and square as possible, because it is the foundation for all your stitching and pressing. Also, it will determine the finished shape of your pocket.

4. Fuse the interfacing to the wrong side of the pocket facing piece.

ATTACH THE POCKET FACING

1. Place the pocket facing and a bag lining piece with right sides of fabric together, matching the CF/CB nick on the top of the pocket facing to the CF/CB nick on the top of the bag lining piece. Align the edges of the fabric, and pin the facing into place.

2. With a small stitch, sew around the stitch line of the facing (stitching just on the fabric side of the cut edge of the interfacing).

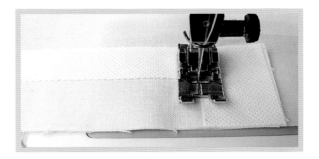

3. Use a fabric marker to draw a line on the wrong side of the facing, ⅜" above the stitch line. (This will be on the fabric that is exposed above the stitch line). We'll call this the seam allowance line.

4. Measure ½" in from each end of the seam allowance line, and place a dot to mark this spot. Draw lines from the dots on the seam allowance line to the corner points of the stitch line, as shown.

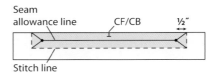

Seam allowance line   CF/CB   ½"

Stitch line

5. Clip off the excess seam allowance from the centerline to the top edges of the pocket facing and bag lining, as shown.

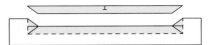

6. Taking extra care not to snip into the stitches, cut the fabric between the corners of the rectangle stitch line to the dots on the seam allowance line.

TIP:

You are less likely to cut stitches if you use a point cutter or scalpel to cut from the corner back toward the dot marking.

7. Press the seam allowances open around the stitch line.

8. Fold the pocket facing up, flipping the seam allowances so that they remain open on the underside. Press the seam flat (from the right side of fabric).

TIP:

Pressing the seam completely open and flat will make it easier to create a sharp, straight edge when the facing is pressed into place.

9. Pull the facing through to the wrong side of the lining piece and press it into place, creating a neat cutaway area where the zipper will sit. Turn and press it from the right side of the lining fabric, too.

INSERT THE ZIPPER

TIPS:

- *You might find the open zipper end easier to manage if you whipstitch the zipper tape together. The easiest way to do this is to set your zigzag stitch on the widest setting and your stitch length close to 0. Hold the zipper tape ends and zigzag them together.*

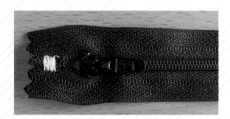

- *Use fusible tape around the edges of the cutaway area on the facing, rather than on the zipper tape. It's then very easy to line up the zipper and press it into place from the right side of fabric. The zipper will then stay put while you sew.*

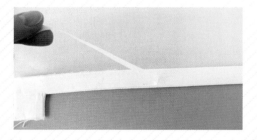

1. Line up the zipper behind the cutaway area with the chain (teeth) of the zipper, ⅛" from the bottom edge. Secure it with pins or fusible tape.

2. Using a zipper foot, topstitch ¹⁄₁₆" from the seamed edge of the cutaway area.

NOTE:

Use a bobbin thread to match the zipper and an upper thread to match the lining fabric.

ATTACH THE POCKET

1. Place the lining piece right side down on the table. Place the pocket right side down over the back of the zipper, with a short edge of the pocket piece aligned with the bottom edge of the pocket facing.

NOTE:

Most of the pocket will extend over the edge of the lining piece. (Yes, it looks wrong, so you'll just have to trust me on this one. In fact, it's all about to get completely counter-intuitive. Honestly, just follow the instructions, and it'll work out fine!)

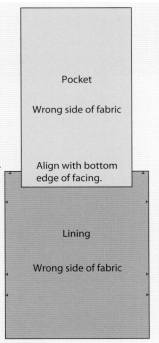

Pocket

Wrong side of fabric

Align with bottom edge of facing.

Lining

Wrong side of fabric

2. Pin, glue, or fuse the bottom edge of the pocket facing and the pocket piece together.

3. Holding the pinned seam allowance, flip the whole lot over to bring the underside of the pocket facing to the top.

4. Stitch as close to the seam as possible to attach the pocket to the pocket facing and the bottom edge of the zipper. Sew the full length of the facing.

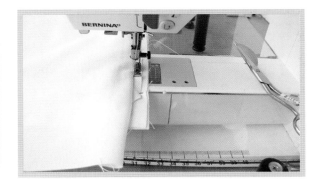

5. Turn the pocket right side out (with the wrong sides of the pocket and lining fabrics together), and press it back from the bottom edge of the zipper.

6. Fold and press the pocket so that the other short edge is in line with the top edge of the lining. Press the fold at the bottom of the pocket bag to make a sharp crease.

7. Turn the lining piece to the right side and stitch ⅟₁₆″ from the top edge of the zipper tape, to attach it to the back of the pocket.

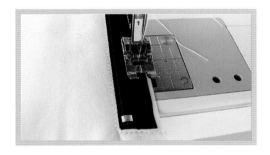

8. Fold the lining pieces back from each end of the zipper, and sew the side seams of the pocket bag.

TIP:

Use a zipper foot to sew the side seams of the pocket bag so that you'll be able to sew very close to the ends of the zipper. The seam allowances will be wider than usual.

Exposed Zipper Pocket

This pocket is similar to the basic method (page 31), but can be placed anywhere on the inside or outside of a bag. My suggestion is to practice the method in the linings of bags—where it won't be obvious—until you're completely confident with it. Then try adding exposed zippers as a design feature on the outside of any bag you please.

CUT AND PREPARE THE POCKET PIECES

1. Use the basic bag pocket (pattern piece #23) to cut a pocket in lining fabric.

2. Cut the zipper pocket 2 facing (pattern piece #11) in lining fabric and also in a flat, non-woven interfacing (such as Vilene S320 or Pellon Craft-Fuse), but do not fuse them together yet.

NOTE:

If you can't find an interfacing that doesn't distort when it's fused, use a light woven interfacing instead. Fuse the interfacing and then copy the pattern markings onto the interfacing, using a ruler and pencil or fabric marker. Skip Steps 3 and 4 and go straight to Attach the Pocket Facing (page 37). The resulting pocket edge may not be as sharp and square as the main instructions will create, but it will be acceptable.

3. Use a sharp pencil (or marker) and ruler to trace the stitch line from the pattern piece onto the non-fusible side of the interfacing. Using a rotary cutter and ruler, cut along the stitch line on the interfacing, removing that section of the interfacing completely.

NOTE:

It's important to cut the interfacing as straight and square as possible; it is the foundation for all your stitching and pressing and will determine the finished shape of your pocket.

4. Fuse the interfacing to the wrong side of the pocket facing piece.

ATTACH THE POCKET FACING

1. Press a crease or draw a line with a Hera or disappearing marker across the bag lining to mark the placement of the exposed zipper. This is usually within the top 3" of the lining.

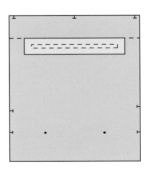

2. With right sides of fabric together, center the pocket facing horizontally on the lining piece, with the top edge of the pocket facing along the crease/ Hera mark.

3. With a small stitch, sew around the stitch line of the pocket facing (stitching just on the fabric side of the cut edge of the interfacing).

4. Measure and draw a line through the center (along the length) of the stitched rectangle. We'll call this line the *seam allowance line*. Measure and mark a dot on the seam allowance line ½" in from each short end of the rectangle stitch line.

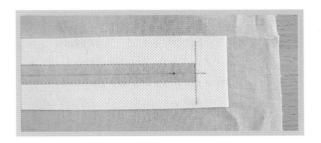

5. Taking extra care not to snip into the stitches, cut the fabric between the corners of the rectangle stitch line to the dots on the seam allowance line.

TIP:

You are less likely to cut stitches if you use a point cutter or scalpel to cut from the corner back toward the dot marking.

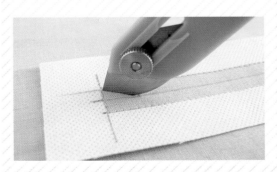

6. Cut an opening along the seam allowance line, between the dots.

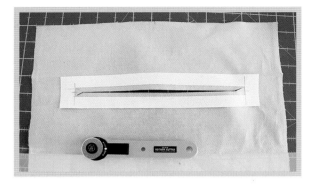

7. Use the point of the iron to press the seam allowances open, around the stitch line. This can be a bit fiddly but is worth the effort because it helps to make a sharp fold along the seamline.

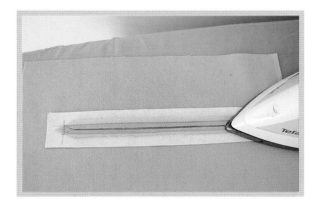

8. Fold the pocket facing up, flipping the seam allowances so that they remain open on the underside. Press the seam flat again, this time from the right side of fabric.

NOTE:

Pressing the seam completely open and flat will make it easier to create a sharp, straight edge when the pocket facing is pressed into place.

9. Pull the pocket facing through to the wrong side of the lining piece and press it into place, creating a neat cutaway "letterbox" shape where the zipper will sit. Turn and press it from the right side of the lining fabric, too.

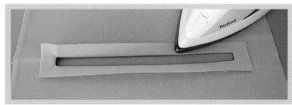

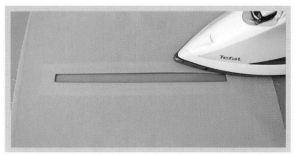

INSERT THE ZIPPER

1. Whipstitch to hold the open ends of the zipper tape together at the open end of the zipper, if desired, and shorten the zipper if necessary.

TIP:

If your zipper is too long, shorten it by whipstitching the chain (teeth) together and trimming off the excess zipper. The whip-stitches can be done with a wide zigzag stitch.

2. Line up the zipper behind the cutaway area with the chain (teeth) of the zipper 1/8" from the bottom edge. Secure it with a pin, tack, glue, or fusible tape.

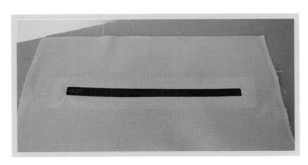

Zipper placement seen from back

TIP:

Use fusible tape around the edges of the cutaway area on the pocket facing, rather than on the zipper tape. It's then very easy to line up the zipper and press it into place from the right side of fabric, and the zipper will stay put while you sew.

3. Using a zipper foot, topstitch 1/16" from the seamed edge of the cutaway area.

TIP:

If you don't want visible stitching on the wrong side of the zipper, use bobbin thread to match the zipper.

ATTACH THE POCKET

1. Place the lining piece right side down on the table. Place the pocket bag right side down over the back of the zipper, with a short edge of the pocket bag aligned with the bottom edge of the pocket facing. Pin, fuse, or glue the bottom edge of the pocket facing and the pocket bag together.

NOTE:

Most of the pocket will extend over the top edge of the lining piece.

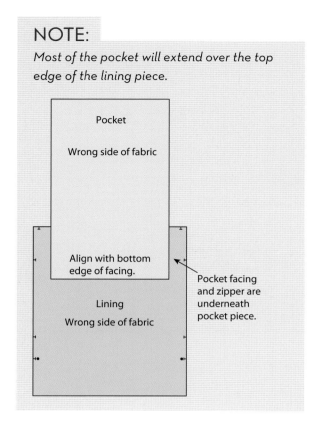

Pocket

Wrong side of fabric

Align with bottom edge of facing.

Lining
Wrong side of fabric

Pocket facing and zipper are underneath pocket piece.

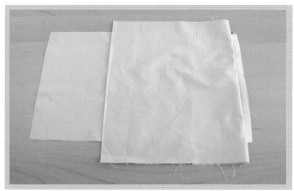

3. Stitch the pocket to the full width of the facing, sewing as close as possible to the seam.

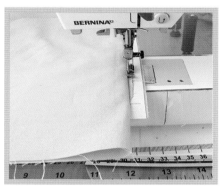

2. Holding the pocket and pocket facing seam allowances together, lift and flip the whole lot over to bring the underside of the pocket facing to the top.

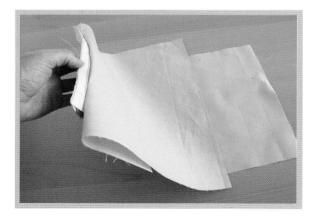

4. Turn the pocket to the right side of fabric (with the wrong sides of the pocket and lining fabrics together), and press it back from the bottom edge of the zipper.

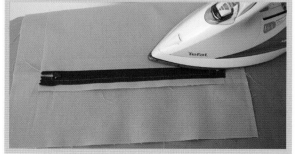

5. Fold and press the pocket so that the other short edge is in line with the top edge of the pocket facing. Press the fold at the bottom of the pocket bag to make a sharp crease.

6. Match the top edge of the pocket to the top edge of the pocket facing. Pin, fuse, or glue it into place.

7. Repeat Steps 2 and 3 to stitch the pocket to the top edge of the pocket facing.

8. Fold the lining pieces back from each end of the zipper, and sew the side seams of the pocket. The width of the seam allowances is ⁵⁄₈".

TIP:

So that you'll be able to sew very close to the ends of the zipper, open the zipper halfway to move the zipper head out of the way, and then use a zipper foot to sew the side seams of the pocket bag.

Zippered Divider Pocket

CUT AND PREPARE THE POCKET PIECES

NOTE:

If the pattern for your project has been slashed and opened or closed along vertical slash line #1, you will need to alter this pattern piece in the same way. If the pattern for your project has been slashed and closed on horizontal slash line #1, you will need to check that the divider pocket will fit between the base corner notch and (at minimum) ³⁄₄" from the top edge of the lining piece. Any excess can simply be trimmed off the bottom of the pocket piece.

1. Cut 4 rectangles of lining fabric (2 pairs of contrasting fabrics is nice) using the divider pocket pattern piece #24. One pair makes the pockets and the other pair makes the lining.

2. Cut a strip of lining fabric 2″ × 6″, and press as if to make a four-fold strap (page 45). This is binding to finish the ends of your zipper.

3. At the open end of the zipper, whipstitch the zipper tape ½″ above the metal stoppers. Trim the ends of the zipper tape off, ⅛″ past the whipstitching.

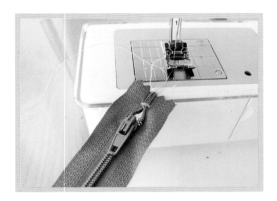

4. Cut the binding in half, and fold half over each end of the zipper tape. Topstitch to attach the folded edges to the zipper.

TIP:

You can use pins to hold the binding in place, but fusible tape, fabric gluestick, or quilt-basting spray makes it much easier.

SEW THE ZIPPER TO THE POCKET

1. Place the zipper facedown on the right side of an outer pocket piece, centered along the top edge. Align the edge of the zipper tape and the top (long) edge of the pocket piece, with the excess binding on the zipper overhanging the edge of the fabric.

2. Open the zipper and begin to stitch the zipper to the fabric ¼″ from the edge of the tape. When you've sewn 3″–4″, lower the needle, raise the presser foot, and close the zipper to move the zipper head out of the way. Continue to sew the full length of the zipper.

3. Match one of the pocket linings to the outer pocket piece with the fabrics right sides together and the zipper sandwiched between.

4. Align the top edge of the pocket lining with the edge of the zipper tape and sew it into place, the full length of the pocket piece, backstitching at each end and following the existing stitch line. Remember to move the zipper head out of the way as you sew past it.

TIP:

You can use pins, fusible tape, or fabric gluestick to hold the lining into place as you stitch.

5. Turn both the outer pocket fabric and the pocket lining to the right side of fabric. Press them back from the zipper, wrong sides together, matching all the raw edges of the outer pocket to the lining.

6. Topstitch 1/16" from the edge of the seam to hold the outer and lining fabrics together. Then stitch another row of top stitching 1/4" from the first.

7. Trim off the excess binding from between the outer and lining layers of the pocket.

8. Repeat Steps 1–6 to attach the other side of the divider pocket to the other side of the zipper.

ATTACH THE POCKET TO THE LINING

1. Press both sides of the pocket and then fold them, lining sides together, so that they are all aligned, one on top of the other. Take care to align the top edges of the pocket, on either side of the bound zipper ends, and pin or fuse them together.

2. Lift the top layer of pocket fabric, and (with a rotary cutter and ruler) trim 3/8" off the bottom edge of the remaining 3 layers. Stitch the 3 layers together 1/4" from the bottom edge to hold them together securely.

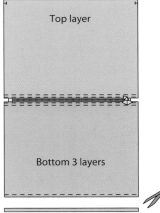

Top layer

Bottom 3 layers

3. Working on the ironing board, place the untrimmed pocket layer under the 3 (stitched together) pocket layers, aligning the side edges. Fold a turning over the untrimmed pocket edge, to encase the other 3 layers, and press it flat.

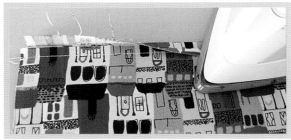

4. Place the pocket right side up (with the raw edge turning to the underside) on the right side of a lining piece. It can be over the top of another pocket. Align the bottom edge of the pocket 1″ above the base corner notches on the lining. Pin, fuse, or glue the bottom and side edges into place.

5. Stitch the sides of the pocket into place, ¼″ from the edge.

6. Topstitch the bottom of the pocket to the lining, ¹⁄₁₆″ from the folded edge, and then top-stitch another row, ¼″ in from the first.

7. At the top of the pocket, bar tack through all layers of fabric to anchor the pocket top to the lining ½″ from each end of the zipper.

THE FLAP

Make the Flap

1. Place the 2 flap (pattern piece #21) pieces right sides together. Beginning at the notch, stitch toward the dot mark near the front edge of the flap.

2. Stop and pivot on the corner dot mark and stitch to the other front corner. Pivot again and then stitch back to the other notch on the back edge of the flap.

3. Remove the interfacing from the seam allowances of the flap, and clip the corners from the ends of the seam to 1¼″ down the sides, including the corner points at the front of the flap. Don't clip too close to the corner stitches!

4. Press the seam allowances open.

5. Turn the flap to the right side and press it flat.

6. Topstitch around the 3 seamed sides of the flap, a generous ¼″ in from the edge.

Curve the Flap

This is a little trick to make the flap sit in a smooth curve over the top of the bag, by reducing the amount of fabric on the underside.

1. Lay the flap on the table with the underside facing upward. Smooth the underside fabric toward the open end at the back of the flap.

2. Fold the lower (front) third of the flap toward the underside. Smooth the fabric of the underside toward the open end of the flap. The underside will overlap the outside by anywhere between 1/16" and 1/2", depending on the thickness of the fabric and interfacings.

3. Turn the folded flap over (so that you can see the outer side). Smooth and pin the outer fabric in place over the overhanging underside fabric, then stitch 1/4" from the back edge of the outer flap piece, to hold the 2 layers of fabric in this position.

4. Trim the overhanging back edge so that the back of the flap is a straight line and the widest part of the stay stitching is within 1/2" of the raw edge.

Attach the Flap

1. Place the outside of the flap against the back of the bag—right sides of fabric together. Pin the center-back notches on the flap to the CB notch on the bag body.

2. Stitch 1/4" from the raw edge of fabric to attach the flap to the top edge of the bag.

STRAPS

There are many ways to construct straps for bags. The two basic techniques are the bagged-out (tube) and four-fold methods. Throughout the projects in this book, you will use these methods several times. You can also substitute any of the more complicated strap designs with these basics, whenever you need a quick and easy option.

Four-Fold Strap

A four-fold strap is used when the strap is too narrow to turn through from the wrong side of fabric. The basic method is as follows:

1. Cut a strap to the required length (plus a seam allowance at each end) by 4 times the (desired) finished strap width.

2. Fold the strap in half (length-wise) with the right side of fabric facing out, and press a crease along the fold.

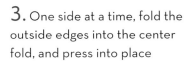

3. One side at a time, fold the outside edges into the center fold, and press into place

4. Fold along the original center crease with the layers sandwiched, and press with steam until all the layers sit flat.

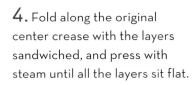

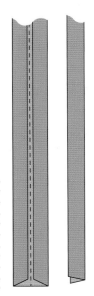

TIP:

Before topstitching, stick the strap together with quilt-basting spray, fabric glue, or fusible tape. To eliminate puckers between rows of top stitching, use a walking foot on your sewing machine, if you have one.

ADDING STRUCTURE TO A FOUR-FOLD STRAP

If you wish to add extra structure to a four-fold strap, you can add interfacing to the full width of the cut strap piece, or you may only interface the middle section or one quarter.

You can also add polyester boning to make the strap sit in a smooth, upright curve. Press the boning to make it lie as flat as possible before putting it inside the folded strap. Use quilt-basting spray or fusible webbing to stick the strap together around the boning before you topstitch the folds of fabric together. You can topstitch multiple rows through the boning if you want to.

ADDING RINGS TO FOUR-FOLD STRAPS

Because a four-fold strap has four layers of fabric, special consideration must be given to the bulk that can build up, especially should you wish to add interfacing or turn the end of the strap over a bag ring. When you turn a raw-edge strap over a ring and stitch it back onto the main strap, you can find yourself with so many thicknesses of fabric that the needle will not penetrate. Here's a simple method for making neat ends on four-fold straps with rings.

1. To reduce bulk, don't use interfacing in the ends of the straps that will be folded. Cut and fuse the interfacing 1″ shorter than the fabric strap anywhere you're inserting a ring.

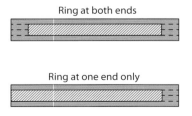

Ring at both ends

Ring at one end only

2. Fold the four-fold strap as usual and press all the creases.

3. At the end of the strap that will be turned over a ring, snip away a square from the inner layer of fabric, leaving 1/8″ along the folded edges. This will reduce the bulk in the end of the strap, but the raw edges of fabric won't show from the outside when the strap is folded and topstitched.

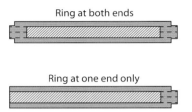

Ring at both ends

Ring at one end only

4. Fold and topstitch all layers of the strap fabric together as usual, and then trim off any rough, raw edges at the ends.

5. Turn the end of the strap through the bag ring, and then fold the last 3/8″ under. Press the turning into place.

6. Use a tailor's awl to poke the raw ends in and to hold the strap end firmly in place as you sew the very edge of the fold line to the strap. Then stitch a box-like shape to enclose the raw ends.

Bagged-Out (Tube) Straps

When a strap is more than 1 1/2″ wide, a four-fold strap unnecessarily uses a lot of fabric. Also considering the issues of bulk (particularly when using heavy fabrics), a four-fold strap is not always the best option for a bag strap. Bagging out a strap—that is, sewing a tube shape from the wrong side of fabric and turning it through—helps to save fabric and reduce bulk. It also offers the opportunity to completely enclose raw ends, which creates tidy, professional-looking straps with bag rings.

1. Cut the strap at twice the desired finished width plus 1″ by the desired length plus 1″. (The 1″ measurements become a ½″ seam allowance at each edge.)

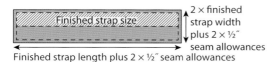

2 × finished strap width plus 2 × ½″ seam allowances

Finished strap length plus 2 × ½″ seam allowances

2. If you are adding interfacing to the strap, consider where bulk may build up (where the strap joins the bag or turns over a ring). Wherever there is a ring at the end of the strap, cut and fuse the interfacing 1″–1½″ shorter than the strap. You may also cut the interfacing without seam allowances on the long edges if you want to avoid too much bulk building up within the seams.

No rings in strap

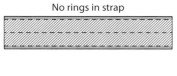

Rings in one end of strap

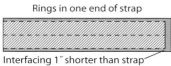

Interfacing 1″ shorter than strap

Rings in both ends of strap

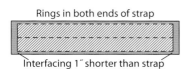

Interfacing 1″ shorter than strap

3. With the right sides of fabric together, fold the strap lengthwise (matching the long edges), and stitch the raw edges together with a ½″ seam allowance. If you plan to have a ring at each end of the strap, leave a gap of 3″–4″ in the middle of the seam, for turning the ends through. If you have no rings or 1 ring, sew the seam the full length of the strap, leaving no gap.

Fold

No rings or rings at one end only

Stitching line

Rings at both ends

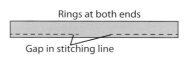

Gap in stitching line

4. Snip the ends of the seam allowances using the corner rule (page 21).

5. Turn the strap so that the seam is at the top, running down the center of the strap, and press the seam allowances open.

TIP:

Use a stick of dowel or quad as a support inside the strap as you press. It will allow you to press the seam very flat and open without the risk of making creases in any other part of the strap.

6. If the strap is to have only 1 ring, stitch across the end that has no interfacing with a ½″ seam allowance, backstitching securely at each folded edge of the strap. If there are to be rings at both ends of the strap, stitch across both ends of the strap in the same manner. If you don't plan to use rings at all, lengthen your machine stitch, and sew across an end without backstitching. (You'll use the stitched ends to help turn the strap through and remove the stitches later.)

TIP:

On any end that is to have a ring, snip off the last ¼" of seam allowance on the corners of the strap at a 45° angle. This will make it easier to make the seam allowance sit flat within the strap once it's turned through (bagged out).

7. Poke the end of the strap in with your thumb or finger and then use a stick of dowel (or a paintbrush, wooden spoon, wooden ruler, or something similar) to push the sewn strap end through the opening at the other end or in the middle of the strap. Don't allow the tube to bunch up on the dowel at the point where it needs to turn through, or it will get stuck (and possibly dislodge the interfacing). Keep the strap as flat as you can, pulling on the turning end in small increments.

TIP:

Wear quilting gloves or any other rubber-palmed gloves (even dishwashing gloves will work) to grip the strap as you pull it over the dowel. It makes the job MUCH easier!

8. If you are not using bag rings, unpick the temporary seam. If you are using rings, gently lift out the corners of the strap with a tailor's awl (or darning needle) to make the corners sharp and square. It's worth taking the time to ensure that the end of the strap is very flat and square, as it will be the stitch guide for the top stitching that encloses the ring in the strap.

9. Check that the seam is flat and open within the tube, and press the strap very flat.

10. If necessary, slipstitch (ladder stitch) to close the opening in the strap.

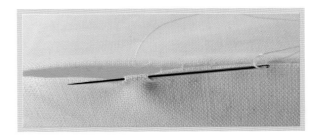

11. Topstitch the strap ⅛" to ¼" from each of the long folded edges (backstitching neatly at each end), and then stitch several more evenly spaced rows to hold all of the layers together.

ADDING RINGS TO BAGGED-OUT STRAPS

1. Loop the closed end through the ring, and fold it back to the underside of the strap.

2. With the end of the strap uppermost on the sewing machine, prepare to stitch as close as possible to the closed short edge to attach it to the main strap. Align the side of the strap with the side of the turned strap end at the point where you will begin to sew, and place it under the machine needle.

3. Hold both threads (page 22) as you begin to sew a neat backstitch. (This will prevent threads from bunching up on the right side of the strap).

4. Use a tailor's awl to align, ease, and hold (one row at a time) the lines of top stitching on the strap end with those on the main strap as you stitch the strap end into place. This will ensure that the presser foot of the machine doesn't stretch the strap end beyond the edges of the main strap and will make it all super-neat.

5. Pivot and sew 4 or 5 stitches toward the bag ring, then pivot and sew another row, parallel to the first row (keeping the edge of your presser foot aligned or parallel with it). Pivot and stitch back to the beginning point, and then do a neat backstitch.

Attach Rings to the Bag

If you want a bag ring to sit more than 4" above the top of the bag, simply construct a second, shorter strap with a closed end and a raw end, and attach it to the other side of the ring as described above. Attach the strap to the bag as described in Step 8 (page 50).

If you want a ring to sit closer to the top of the bag, make O-ring loops or tabs. Methods include a four-fold strap for lighter fabrics and narrower straps, and this one, which suits most fabric types and is simple enough for beginner sewing skills.

1. For each ring, cut a small strap that is twice the desired width plus 1" by twice the desired length plus 1".

2. If you are using quilting-weight fabric, cut and fuse interfacing the full length of the strap but not on the lengthwise seam allowances. If you are using a fabric that is heavier than quilting weight, cut a strip of interfacing that is the actual finished width of the loop, and fuse down the center of the strap.

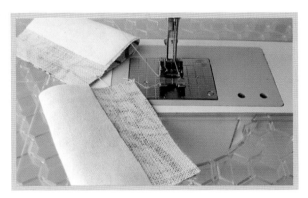

3. With the right sides of fabric together, fold the straps lengthwise and stitch the raw edges together with a ½" seam allowance.

4. Clip the seam allowances using the corner rule, and press them open (using a dowel or wooden spoon as support inside the strap).

5. Turn the strap through to the right side, move the seam to the center, and press the strap flat from both sides.

6. Topstitch along both sides of the strap, ⅛″ to ¼″ from the edge, and then stitch a few more evenly spaced rows between.

7. Fold the strap through the bag ring, with the seam on the inside of the fold. Match together the raw ends to make the strap into a loop. Stitch the raw ends together ¼″ from the ends, taking particular care to align the side edges.

8. Place the loops right (the prettiest) side down on the right side of the bag, aligning the raw edges with the top edges of the bag. Stitch the loops into place, ¼″ from the edge. When you attach the facing to the top edge of the bag, the raw edges will be caught and hidden by the seam.

Adjustable Straps

Follow the instructions for the four-fold strap with a ring at each end (page 46) or the bagged-out straps with rings at both ends (page 47), but don't attach the rings yet. Also make O-ring loops and attach them to O-rings for your adjustable strap

1. Thread an end of the strap over the center bar on a slide adjuster, folding it over the bar about 2″ from the strap end. On a four-fold strap, fold the end of the strap under ½″ as you bring it to the back of the main strap. For a bagged-out strap, you will not have to fold the end under.

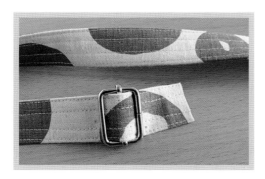

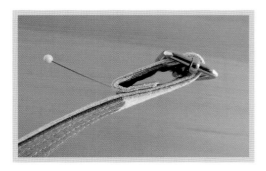

2. Using a tailor's awl to hold the folded strap end in place on the underside of the strap, topstitch along the fold. Pivot and, using the awl to poke in any stray raw strap ends, stitch ½" along the side of the strap, toward the slide adjuster. Pivot and stitch across the strap to the other side, again poking in stray strap ends with the tailor's awl. Pivot and stitch along the edge of the strap, back to the folded edge. (With some presser feet, you may have to do this in reverse if the back of the foot hits the slide adjuster.) Backstitch securely.

3. With the underside of the shoulder strap (the side with the turned end of the strap) facing upward, thread the other end of the shoulder strap through an O-ring (which is attached to the O-ring loop).

4. Fold the raw end of the strap and thread it through the slide adjuster.

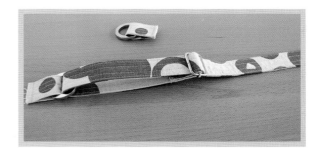

5. Thread the end of the shoulder strap through the other O-ring. Fold the strap about 2½" from the end with the O-ring in the fold, taking care to check that the right side of the strap is facing outward.

Basic Bag-Making Techniques   51

6. On a four-fold strap, turn under the last ½" of the raw end (a bagged-out strap will not have a raw end). Stitch the end to the strap as in Step 2, using a tailor's awl to hold everything in place as you stitch a rectangular shape.

7. With the right side of the shoulder strap facing the right side of the bag, match the raw ends of each O-ring loop to the desired position on the top edge of the bag.

8. Stitch the O-ring loops into place, ¼" from the top edge.

BAG BASES

As with everything relating to bag construction, there are many ways to make a bag base.

Internal (Textile) Base Support

The simplest bag base is an internal base made using a heavy craft interfacing (such as Timtex, Peltex, or fast2fuse).

This 100% textile base gives structure without sharp edges. It is ideal for bags that will be worn against the body, allows the bag to be washed and ironed, and is easy to manage around a sewing machine. The density and structure of the base can be altered by layering interfacing around it until it has your preferred firmness.

1. Cut the base interfacing using the bag base support (pattern piece #7).

2. Cut a piece of lightweight fusible interfacing 1½" longer than the long edges by 3 times the length of the short edges of the base support piece.

3. Place the bag base support on the adhesive side of the fusible interfacing, with the length of the base centered between the 2 longer edges of the interfacing. Leave a ¾" seam allowance of interfacing on either side of the support piece.

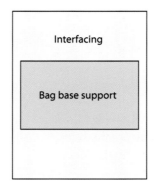

Interfacing

Bag base support

4. Wrap the interfacing smoothly around the base support (it will overlap), and fuse all the layers together. You can add more layers of interfacing until you have as much structure as you want in the base.

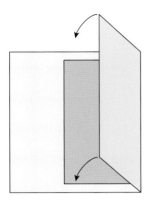

5. Sew around the edges and sew an X shape through the center of the bag base. This doesn't have to be neat because nobody will ever see it. The stitching is simply to reinforce the adhesive that holds the base together.

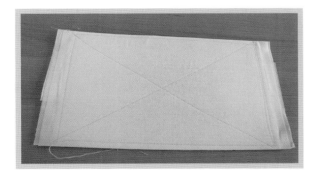

6. Center the base support between the base seams of the side panels, and pin the seam allowances together to hold it in place.

7. Sew the seam allowances of the bag base to the seam allowances of the bag, ¼" from the raw edges of bag fabric.

External Textile Bag Base

This bag base involves adding a separate, structured piece to the outside of the bag, which creates a clean fold to define the bottom edge of the bag. It holds the shape of the bag base, yet is flexible enough to carry comfortably against the body.

This is a good introduction to working with stiffer bag-support materials. It can be added to any of the bag projects in this book, even if the instructions suggest an internal base, and can be adapted to suit other bags.

1. Use the bag base (pattern piece #6) to cut the main or contrast fabric. Cut the bag base support (pattern piece #7) in Peltex 71 or 72 or fast2fuse.

TIP:

If you'd like to add extra structure or smooth the surface of the bag base, also cut the bag base support (pattern piece #7) in firm fusible interfacing (such as Vilene 320 or Pellon Craft-Fuse), and fuse it to the fabric before the Peltex or fast2fuse (see Step 2).

2. Place the Peltex/fast2fuse on the wrong side of fabric and center it (so you can see an even seam allowance of fabric around the edges). Then press from both sides of the fabric until the base support is firmly fused in place.

Bag base   Wrong side of fabric

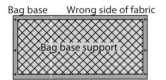

Bag base support

NOTE:

If using a double-sided fusible base material, such as fast2fuse or Peltex 72, cover the exposed adhesive with a Teflon appliqué mat or parchment paper. If using Peltex 71, cover the nonadhesive side with a fabric pressing cloth as you press.

3. Using the long edges of the Peltex/fast2fuse as a folding edge, turn the long edges of the base piece over the edges of the Peltex/fast2fuse, and press them to fuse. Do not fold the short ends of the base (these will go into the seams at the base of the side panels). If you're using Peltex 71, add a narrow strip of fusible tape to hold the folded edges in place.

Fold

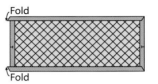

Fold

4. Trim the corners of the long edge seam allowances using the corner rule, from the seam allowance notches on the short ends to just over an inch down the outside edge.

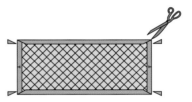

5. Sew the base seam of the bag body, and clip and press the seam allowances open.

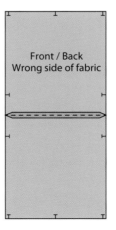

Front / Back
Wrong side of fabric

6. Place the bag base right side up over the right side of the base seam on the bag body, aligning the base seam with the center notches on the raw edges of the textile base.

TIP:

Use quilt-basting spray to hold the base in place on the bag body.

7. Topstitch the base to the bag body, 1/16″ from the long, folded edges.

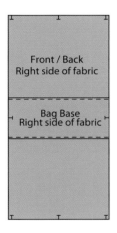

Front / Back
Right side of fabric

Bag Base
Right side of fabric

8. Continue to construct the bag, following the project instructions.

Structured External Base with Purse Feet

This base is made with template plastic as the main support. The springy flexibility of template plastic allows you to construct the bag using a normal domestic sewing machine and turn the bag through to the right side, yet it holds a flat shape when it's finished. The addition of purse feet in the base is optional, but they help to protect the base of the bag from wear and tear.

CUT THE BAG BASE PIECES

1. Cut the bag base (pattern piece #6) in the main or contrast fabric.

2. Cut the bag base support (pattern piece #7) in sturdy pelmet interfacing (Vilene S520 or Pellon 520F Deco-Fuse). If you plan to add purse feet, mark the purse feet placements on the nonadhesive side of the interfacing.

TIP:

Use a quilting ruler and pencil to measure and draw feet placement lines in from each edge of the pelmet interfacing, and then draw another through the center (across the width). Where the lines intersect is where the feet will sit. The distance between the interfacing edge and the feet placement lines will depend on the size of the bag, and distances are indicated in the individual project instructions.

3. Trace the bag base support (pattern piece #7) onto template/stencil plastic and cut it out. Cut on the inside of the line so that, if anything, the template plastic is slightly smaller than the pelmet interfacing base piece.

4. Center the interfacing on the wrong side of the base fabric (you should be able to see the base fabric seam allowances around the interfacing), and fuse it into place.

Bag Base
Wrong side of fabric

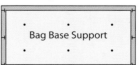

Bag Base Support

PREPARE FOR PURSE FEET

(Skip to Construct the Bag Base, below, if not using purse feet)

1. Working on a cutting board or mat, place the template plastic over the top of the interfacing on the bag base.

TIP:

You can use gluestick (the type that is used for paper crafts) to hold the template plastic in place on the back of the interfacing, or you can tape all layers to the cutting board.

2. Punch holes through all the layers of plastic and fabric, using a saddler's punch and mallet.

CONSTRUCT THE BAG BASE

1. Remove the template plastic from the base for now.

2. Press the long edges of the seam allowances inward, creasing the fabric sharply over the hard edge of the interfacing.

3. Trim the corners of the long-edge seam allowances using the corner rule, from the seam allowance notches on the short ends to just over an inch down the outside edge.

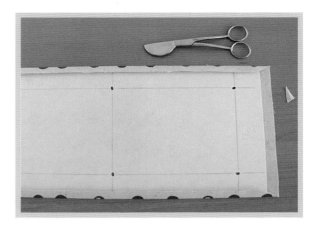

4. Slide the template plastic into place over the interfacing and under the seam allowances of the bag base. If you have punched holes for purse feet in the template plastic, align the holes with the holes on the base fabric.

5. If using purse feet, push the prongs of the feet through from the right side of fabric to the template plastic side. Splay the prongs apart on the template plastic.

6. Fold each of the corners of the short-end seam allowance at a 45° angle, aligning what was the outer folded edge with the end of the interfacing and template plastic. You can press and pin this into place, but a fabric gluestick works better to hold the folds.

4. Topstitch the base to the bag body, 1/16" from the folded edge; remove the tape as the sewing machine needle approaches it. An edge-stitching presser foot can make it easier to keep this stitching straight.

5. At the short ends of the base, topstitch 1/16" from the edge along the angled fold of the seam allowances and then pivot and stitch 1/4" in from the raw edge of fabric to attach the seam allowances of the base to the bag body seam allowances.

TIP:

Run a fabric gluestick along the long edges of the template plastic, and stick the seam allowances to the plastic.

ATTACH THE BASE TO THE BAG

1. Sew the base seam of the bag body, and clip and press the seam allowances open, as in the Basic Bag instructions (page 66).

2. Place the bag base on the right side of fabric over the base seam of the bag body. Match the center notches on the seam allowances with the base seam on the bag, and align the raw edges of fabric.

3. Pin the seam allowances of the bag and base together, and use quilt-basting spray or tape to hold the base to the bag body.

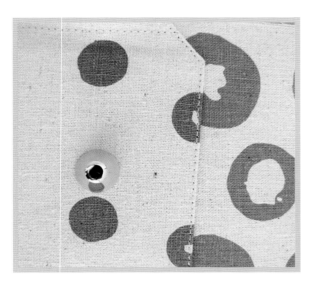

6. Continue to construct the bag, following the project instructions. You can squeeze the sides of the base together as you sew the side seams of the bag. It's a little awkward at first, but the more you do it, the easier it gets.

BAG CLOSURES

Magnetic Snap

1. Take the back plate of a magnetic snap, and place the center hole over the placement mark on the facing. Mark the fabric with 2 little lines, using the back plate as a template.

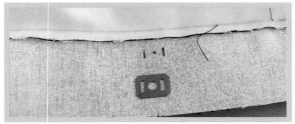

2. Use very sharp scissors, a point cutter, or a scalpel to cut 2 tiny slits through these lines. Take care to err on the side of *too small* a slit, rather than too large.

3. Push the prongs of the magnetic catches from the right side of the fabric, through the little incisions, to the back (interfacing side) of the fabric.

NOTE:

The thick (magnet) side of the snap is usually on the back of the bag and the flat side on the front. On a bag flap, the thick side goes on the bag body and the flat side on the flap.

4. To protect the fabric of the facing from the sharp edges of the back plate, cut a square of Peltex, fast2fuse, or Timtex a little bigger than the back plate; cut slits to match the prongs on the clasp; and push it over the prongs and onto the back of the facing.

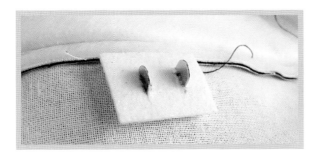

5. Place the back plate over the prongs and fold the prongs inward. Tap the prongs with a hammer to make them sit flat.

TIP:

By folding the prongs inward, you protect the fabric surrounding the clip from being torn by the prongs.

6. The sharp edges of the prongs can create a lump or, even worse, cut through the fabric. To smooth over the back of the magnetic snap, fuse a piece of fast2fuse and a layer of other interfacing over the back of the clip and onto the surrounding fabric. (Alternatively, use Vilene S520, Deco-Fuse, or several layers of Vilene S320, and you won't need the second layer of interfacing.)

7. Mark a stitch line with a Hera marker or fabric marker, and using the zipper foot, topstitch around the snap from the right side of the facing fabric. Do not stitch through to the outer bag.

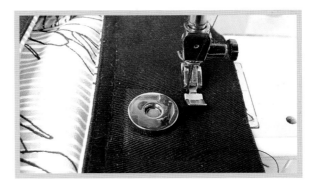

8. Repeat for the other side of the snap.

Zippered Gusset

This method can be used on any bag with a facing and lining. The essential ingredient here is a good interfacing that fuses easily without distorting and has a flat (paper-like) finish. If you can find it, Vilene S320 is perfect for this. It creates a crisp, clean effect and makes it very easy to be accurate and neat.

CUT AND FUSE THE PIECES

1. The individual projects have the measurements to cut the interfacing, which is the starting point for constructing the zipper gusset this way. Cut the interfacing to size, taking particular care to keep the rectangles accurate and square—this is key to the success of the finished zipper gusset.

2. Fuse 1 of the interfacing pieces to the wrong side of some spare main fabric and 1 piece to the wrong side of some lining fabric, leaving enough space around each to add ½″ seam allowances.

3. Cut the gusset pieces on the outer and lining fabrics, adding ¼″ seam allowances onto each of the long sides and ½″ seam allowances to the short sides of the interfacing.

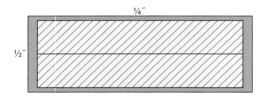

> ## NOTE:
> *Adding accurate seam allowances is very easy with a quilting ruler and rotary cutter.*

4. Cut both gusset pieces in half lengthwise to make 2 long rectangles in both the lining and outer fabrics.

CONSTRUCT THE ZIPPER GUSSET

1. On the wrong side of 1 of the outer zipper gussets, on the edge that has the ¼″ seam allowance of fabric, measure and mark a line 1″ from a short end. Mark this position with a pin (or a small mark in the seam allowance on the right side of the gusset).

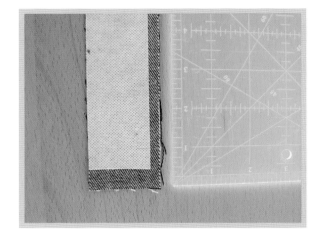

2. Place the zipper facedown on the right side of this zipper gusset. Align the edge of the zipper tape with the ¼″ seam allowance of the gusset, with the zipper stopper (at the opening end of the zipper) even with the 1″ mark.

3. At the other end of the gusset, place a pin at the end of the interfacing (which is fused to the wrong side of fabric). The pin should be ½″ short of the end of the gusset.

4. Open the zipper fully and use pins, fusible tape, or fabric gluestick to hold the zipper tape in place. Remember to keep 1 pin at the 1" mark and another even with the end of the interfacing at the other end.

5. Beginning at the 1" mark (or pin), backstitch and stitch a generous 1/4" from the edge of the zipper tape, stopping at the pin at the other end of the gusset. Do not cross over the pins. Backstitch securely.

This shows the placement of stitches when viewed from the back side.

6. At the open end of the zipper, fold the loose end of the zipper tape over the metal stopper, and twist it off the edge of the 1/4" seam allowance. The idea is to get as much of the tape as possible off the seam allowances on the gusset. Tack or baste the zipper tape ends in place.

7. Pin or glue a lining piece right side down over the top of the zipper tape you just stitched, aligning the 1/4" fabric seam allowance with the zipper tape. The zipper will be sandwiched between the 2 gusset pieces.

8. Backstitch and sew the lining into place, following the existing line of stitching, but sew past the folded end of the zipper tape to the end of the interfacing. Pivot and sew around the short end (as close as possible to the edge of the interfacing without catching it in the seam). Backstitch securely.

9. Clip the seam allowances at the short end of the gusset to a point in the middle, and trim the corner of the zipper seam allowance to 1/2" from the corner.

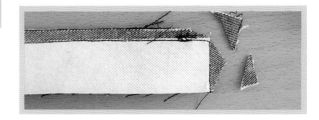

10. Turn the gusset pieces right side out, paying particular attention to making the corner point a sharp square shape. Press the outer and lining pieces away from the zipper, with all edges aligned.

TIP:

Use a tailor's awl to gently lift out the corner points from the right side of fabric (but don't pull the awl all the way through or you will tear the fabric).

11. At the opposite short end of the gusset (where the zipper continues past it), fuse fusible tape along the edge of the interfacing and onto the ¼" seam allowance of the outer gusset piece. Leave the backing paper on.

12. Use the backing paper as a folding line, fold the short-end seam allowances toward the interfacing side of fabric, and press them into place.

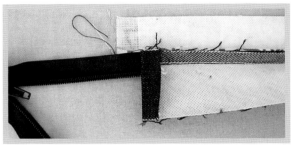

13. Clip the corners of the turned seam allowance from the ends of the crease (at the edge of the tape) to a point in the middle.

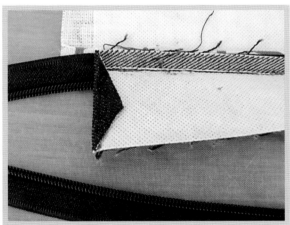

14. Fold and press the seam allowance back over the tape, and then remove the backing paper. While the adhesive is still warm, finger-press the seam allowance to stick it down. Fold the raw edge corners above the seam on the zipper tape in toward the center so they won't show on the edge of the finished gusset. You may need extra tape or a fabric gluestick to hold the raw edge corners down.

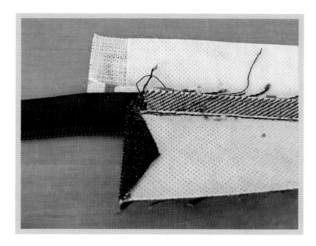

15. Repeat Steps 11–14 for the lining piece, taking care to neatly match the folded edges of the outer fabric and lining.

16. Use a 1″ strip of fusible webbing to stick the outer and lining pieces wrong sides together, aligning the folded and raw edges.

17. Repeat Steps 1–16 to attach the other side of the zipper gusset, checking throughout that both halves of the gusset align.

18. Topstitch a generous 1/16″ from the edge around each of the zipper gusset pieces. On the 2 short ends and along the zipper side of each gusset piece, stitch a second row of top stitching 1/4″ in from the first row.

MAKE THE ZIPPER TAB

You can use any stiff interfacing as a base for zipper tabs.

1. Some projects will give you the measurements to cut the interfacing (the starting point) for the zipper tab. If not specified, cut a rectangle of interfacing 1/2″ wider than the zipper and 3″ long. Cut the interfacing and fuse it to the wrong side of a scrap of fabric.

2. Trim the seam allowances back to 3/8″ on the long edges and 1/2″ on the short ends.

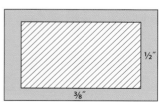

3. Fuse a line of fusible tape along each of the long edges of the interfacing, extending it onto the seam allowances at each of the short ends.

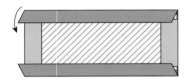

4. Turn and press the fabric over the edges of the interfacing on both of the long sides.

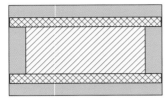

5. Clip the corners of the seam allowances from the end of each crease to ½" down the raw edge of fabric.

6. Peel the backing paper off the fusible tape, turn the tab right side of fabric upward on an appliqué mat or baking parchment, and press to stick the seam allowances in place on the wrong side of fabric.

7. While the webbing is still warm, turn in the raw edge corners at each end of the tab, leaving a ⅛" gap between the folded ends and the edge of the interfacing. This gap will allow the end to turn over neatly to make sharp corner points.

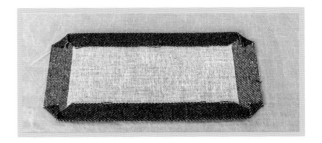

8. Fold and press the short-end seam allowances over the edge of the interfacing, using fusible tape or fabric gluestick to hold them in place.

9. Use fusible webbing or quilt-basting spray on the wrong side of the tab. Fold and press the tab (right side out) around the end of the zipper, and fuse or glue it.

10. Topstitch around the tab, as close to the edge as you can neatly sew, and then stitch another row of top stitching ¼" in from the first.

NOTE:

You won't be able to stitch over the end of a chunky metal or plastic zipper chain, but stitch as close to it as you can, and then pivot to stitch the second row of top stitching.

ATTACH THE ZIPPER GUSSET TO THE BAG

1. Measure and mark the halfway point on both of the raw seam allowance edges of the gusset, and then open the zipper.

2. With the bag wrong side out, put any straps and flaps inside the body of the bag. Turn the facing upward so that it sits upright above the top of the bag, with the raw edge at the very top.

3. Match the center nick on the facing to the center mark on the zipper gusset, right sides together. Working from the center out, line up the raw edges of the facing and gusset, and pin them into place. (Use bulldog clips instead of pins if you are working with PVC/vinyl or leather).

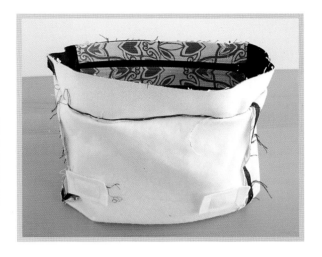

4. Stitch the gusset into place, ³/₈" in from the edge.

5. Repeat Steps 1–4 for the other side of the gusset and bag.

6. Attach the lining to the bag. The gusset is now sandwiched between the facing and the lining.

BASIC BAG

FINISHED BAG: 12½" × 13¾" × 7½"

This bag is the building block from which all of the bags in this book are derived. In order to familiarize yourself with the basic construction techniques used throughout the projects, make this bag as a simple shopping tote for yourself.

Your first bag should never be in your best fabric, and you should never expect it to be perfect. Even after years of making all sorts of bags and purses, my second attempt at making anything always produces better results than the first. Confidence and knowing what lies ahead take the stress out of trying something new, and fewer mistakes are made along the way.

Even if you are confident of your sewing skills, it's still a good idea to quickly make up this bag

to familiarize yourself with the methods used. If you're looking for more of a challenge, you could fancy it up with a more challenging fabric (such as a laminate), or you could add extra features from the Basic Bag-Making Techniques section (page 25) to design your own variation.

Once you have an understanding of how the construction process works, you can vary the basic design endlessly.

PATTERN PIECES

- Front/Back bag body (pattern piece #1)
- Side panel (pattern piece #2)
- Facing (pattern piece #5)
- Lining (pattern piece #3)
- Lining side panel (pattern piece #4)
- Zipper pocket 1 facing (pattern piece #9)
- Compartment pocket (pattern piece #8)
- Basic bag pocket (pattern piece #23)
- Bag base support (pattern piece #7)
- Straps will be measured and cut according to instructions.

MATERIALS

- 1¼ yards quilting- or decor-weight fabric for outer bag*
- 1 yard quilting-weight fabric for lining
- 2¼ yards medium-weight fusible woven interfacing
- 2" × 11" nonwoven fusible interfacing (Vilene S320 or Pellon Craft-Fuse) for zipper pocket facing
- 8" × 13" fast2fuse, Peltex 71/72, or Timtex for bag base support
- 1 magnetic snap ¾"
- 1 zipper 8" to match lining fabric
- Thread to match outer and lining fabrics

I used "Flutter" by Riley Blake.

PREPARE THE BAG PIECES

1. Roughly cut the interfacing (½″ bigger) around the pattern pieces for the bag body, side panel, and facing. Fuse the interfacing to the wrong side of the outer fabric. (See Block Fusing, page 20).

2. Cut 2 of each of these pieces: bag body, side panel, and facing.

3. Mark the pattern notches with ⅛″ nicks in the fabric. Mark the dots on the interfacing side of the side panel pieces with a fabric marker, pencil, or chalk.

4. Cut 2 each of the lining and lining side panel pieces in lining fabric, and snip all the pattern notches with ⅛″ nicks.

5. Cut the basic bag pocket, zipper pocket 1 facing, and the compartment pocket in lining fabric.

6. Cut 2 straps 4″ × 26″ from the main fabric. Cut 2 interfacing pieces 3″ × 26″, and fuse them, centered on the wrong side of the strap fabric.

7. Cut the base support from the fast2fuse, Peltex, or Timtex.

TIP:

If you take care to fuse, cut, and mark the bag pieces accurately, the whole thing will come together without the unnecessary trouble of trying to make badly cut pieces fit. What looks like the long way around is actually the shortcut!

SEW THE BAG BODY

The Base Seam

1. Place the bag body pieces right sides together. Matching the seam allowance nicks on the base seam, sew the base seam with a ½″ seam allowance, backstitching at each end.

2. Clip the seam allowances at both ends of the seam to 1¼″ down the side edges, using the corner rule (page 21), and press the seam allowances open.

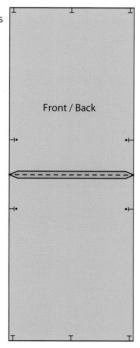

The Side Panels

1. Place a side panel and a bag body piece right sides together, matching the side seam. Align the notches at the top edges, and pin the dot at the corner of the side panel to the corresponding dot on the bag body.

2. Backstitch and begin sewing the side seam from the top edge, with a ½″ seam allowance. Slow down as you reach the corner point so that you can stop exactly on the dot. When you reach the dot, backstitch securely.

3. Peel and trim the interfacing off the last 1″–2″ of the seam allowance at the top of the side seam. Then trim the seam allowances to 1¼″ down the edge of the seam allowance (see the corner rule, page 21). This will reduce bulk in the seam where it attaches to the facing.

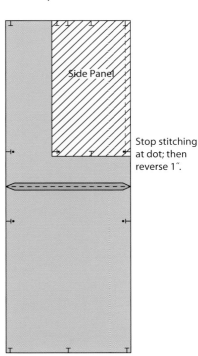

Stop stitching at dot; then reverse 1″.

NOTE:

When following these instructions for other projects in the book, it may be necessary to remove the interfacing from the entire seam allowance (see Reducing Bulk, page 20). If you are using light fabric and interfacing to make this as a basic shopping bag, removing 1″–2″ is enough.

4. Using your sharpest scissors, snip from the notch at the base corner of the bag body to a scant 1/16″ from the end of the side seam. Take care not to cut the stitches or beyond them.

5. Repeat Steps 1–4 to attach the other side of this side panel to the other bag body piece.

6. Repeat Steps 1–5 to attach the other side panel. Press these 4 seams open. (Fig. A)

7. Align the base seam of the side panel with the base seam section of the bag body. The snipped corner points will allow the fabric to turn the corner. Pin the base seam of the bag body to the notch in the center of the side panel, and align the raw edges of the seam allowances. Pin at the corner points, too, if necessary. (Fig. B)

8. Sew the base seam of the side panel to the bag body with a ½" seam allowance, backstitching securely at each end. Stitch a little around each of the corner points to the side seam. (Fig. C & D)

9. At each of the base corner points, trim from ¹⁄₁₆" away from the corner stitches to a generous 1" down the edge of each seam allowance. (Fig. E)

10. Repeat Steps 7–9 for the other side panel base seam.

A.

B.

C.

D.

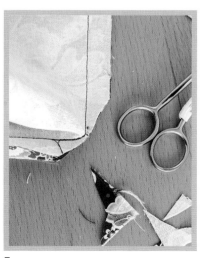

E.

Make the Straps

Using the 4″ × 26″ strap pieces, follow the instructions for bagged-out straps with no rings (page 46). If you wish to make alternate, two-fabric straps instead, follow the cutting and assembly instructions on page 77.

Attach the Straps

1. Measure and snip a notch 2½″ on either side of the CF/CB notch on the front and back bag body pieces.

2. Match 1 edge of a strap end to the notch as you align the raw end to the top of the bag. Pin the strap end to the bag.

3. Curl the strap around (without twisting) to the top of the bag, matching the other end. Match the edge of the strap to the notch and the raw edge of the strap end to the raw edge of the bag. Pin it into place.

4. Repeat Steps 1–3 to attach the other strap to the other side of the bag, and then stitch all the ends in place, ¼″ from the raw edge.

MAKE THE FACING

1. Place the facing pieces right sides together, and align the notches on the short ends.

2. Stitch the side seams on the short ends, backstitching at the end of each seam.

3. Trim the interfacing from the seam allowances, clip the corners using the corner rule, and press the seams open.

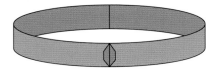

4. Place the facing around the top edge of the bag, right sides of fabric together and aligning the notches and seams. Stitch with a ½″ seam allowance around the top.

5. If you need to reduce bulk in the seams (some projects will instruct you to do this), you can trim interfacing or fleece off the seam allowances.

UNDERSTITCH THE FACING

This is a vital part of making the top of the bag sit in a clean, sharp line, and it makes it much easier to fold the facing into place. Test it. Before you start understitching, try folding the facing back toward the inside of the bag, and then do the under stitching and try folding it again. You'll then see what a difference it makes.

1. Turn the facing to the right side of fabric, so that you can see the right side of the seam. Don't press the seam.

2. With the right side of fabric uppermost on the machine, fold all the seam allowances to the facing side, and line up the machine needle 1/16" from the seam, on the facing side. The seam allowances will be caught in the stitches. Begin to stitch, using the fingers on both hands to flatten the seam in front of the needle. Use your thumb on the underside to check that the seam allowances stay flat and underneath the facing.

NOTE:

When the top of the bag is curved, trim away 1/4" of the seam allowance so the remaining seam allowances will sit flat.
When the top of the bag is a straight line, don't trim the seam allowances; they'll act as a support structure within the top edge to help the bag hold its shape.

TOPSTITCH THE FACING

1. Fold the facing (right side facing out) toward the inside of the bag. Use the under-stitched edge to push the seam to the very top edge of the bag, and press the seam and the facing flat.

2. Topstitch ¼″ around the top edge of the bag. This will hold all the layers of fabric and seam allowance together and give the bag a crisp, finished edge.

INSERT THE MAGNETIC SNAP

Follow the instructions for inserting a magnetic snap (page 58).

MAKE AND ATTACH THE BASE

Follow the instructions in Internal (Textile) Base Support (page 52) to make and attach the base.

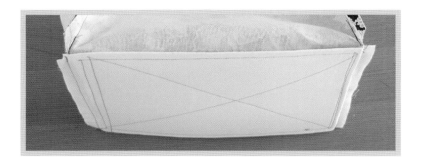

CONSTRUCT THE POCKETS

Follow the instructions for the Basic Zipper Pocket (page 31) and Compartment Pocket (page 30).

SEW THE LINING

1. Place the main (bag body) lining pieces right sides together. Sew the ends of the base seam with a ½" seam allowance, leaving a gap of 8"–10" in the middle and backstitching at each end of each seam. This gap will be where the bag is turned through to the right side when it's finished.

2. Clip the seam allowances using the corner rule (page 21), and press the seam allowances open, including the part that isn't sewn together.

3. Match the side seams of a lining side panel and a lining piece, right sides together. Align the notches at the top edges, and pin the dot at the corner of the side panel to the corresponding dot on the bag body.

4. With the main (bag body) lining piece uppermost on the machine, backstitch and begin sewing the seam from the top edge, with a ½" seam allowance. Slow down as you reach the corner point so that you can stop exactly on the dot. When you reach the dot, reverse stitch backward (or pivot 180° and sew forward) for 1" back over the seam.

5. Lift the presser foot and, with *sharp* scissors, snip the seam allowance from the notch to a whisker (about ¹⁄₃₂") away from the dot. Take care not to cut the stitch or beyond it.

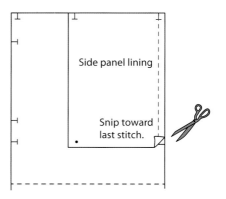

Side panel lining

Snip toward last stitch.

6. Stitch back toward the dot, along the same seamline. When you reach the dot, put your needle down and lift up the presser foot. Open up the snipped seam allowance, and align the base section of the bag body with the base of the side panel. Align the notch on the side panel with the base seam, and pin the other corner dots together.

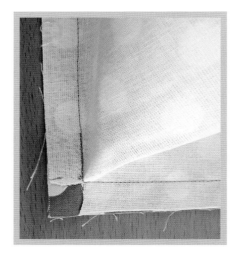

7. Stitch to the dot, reverse 1", and snip the seam again. Align the side seams and stitch to the top edge of the lining. Backstitch to secure the end of the seam.

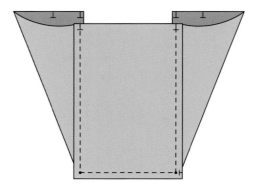

8. Clip the corners of the seam allowances to reduce bulk.

9. Repeat Steps 3–8 to attach the other side panel, and press all the seams open.

ATTACH THE LINING

1. With the bag inside out, turn the lining so that the right side of fabric is to the outside.

2. Fold up the facing so that the raw edge is sitting upward at the top of the bag.

3. Put the lining inside the bag (right sides together). Align the top edge of the lining with the raw edges of the facing, matching the notches and seams. Pin the lining into place.

TIP:

Check that the pockets are sitting against the front and back of the bag, as they're intended to be on the finished bag. If a pocket is to be on the back lining of the bag, it needs to be facing the back of the bag as you stitch the lining into place.

4. Stitch the lining to the facing with a ½″ seam allowance. Swap to a zipper foot to sew past the zipper of the basic zippered pocket.

5. Turn the bag through to the right side through the gap in the base seam of the lining.

FINISH THE LINING

This will hold the lining firmly inside the bag.

1. Pull 1 of the bottom corners of the bag (the base seam of the side panel) through the gap in the lining. Pull the corresponding base seam of the lining through the gap, and pin the raw edges of the seam allowances.

2. Stitch the base seam allowances of the base support, lining, and bag together (by machine or by hand), ¼" from the raw edges.

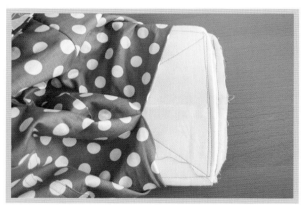

3. Repeat Steps 1 and 2 for the other corner of the bag.

4. Close the gap in the lining with slip stitch/ ladder stitch.

ALTERNATE TWO-FABRIC STRAPS

PREPARE THE STRAP PIECES

1. Cut 2 straps 2¼″ × 26″ from the main fabric.

2. Cut strips of light interfacing and fusible webbing 1½″ × 23″ for each of the main fabric strap pieces.

TIP:

The interfacing and the paper backing on the webbing provide a sharp edge to use as a fold line for the seam allowances. If you take care to cut straight, it will be easy to make a sharp, straight strap edge.

3. Fuse the interfacing on the wrong side of the main fabric straps, centered evenly (with seam allowances showing around the edges of the interfacing). Fuse the fusible webbing on top of the interfacing, and leave the backing paper on (page 19).

4. Cut 2 straps 2¼″ × 24″ from the contrast fabric.

5. Cut strips of fusible webbing 1½″ × 24″ for each of the contrast fabric strap pieces. On the last 2″ at the end of each fusible webbing strap, taper the ends to ¼″ narrower than the rest of the strap.

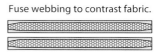

Fusible webbing 1½″ × 24″

6. Fuse the webbing to the wrong side of fabric, along the center of the contrast fabric straps. Leave the backing paper on.

Fuse webbing to contrast fabric.

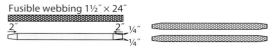

ASSEMBLE THE STRAPS

1. On the 2 main strap pieces, turn the seam allowances of the long edges over the webbing's backing paper, and press them flat and into place. Make sure that the crease is sharp and straight before proceeding. (It's worth taking care here.)

Fold seam allowances toward wrong side.

2. On the long sides of the main fabric straps, trim the seam allowances, using the corner rule (page 21), from the top of the crease at each end to ¾″ down the outer edge of the strap.

Clip the corners of seam allowances.

3. Remove the paper backing from each of the straps, and carefully press the seam allowances to fuse them into place.

Use an appliqué mat to protect your ironing board from the webbing, and take care to avoid touching the webbing with your iron. You may even prefer to use an old iron while you're working with fusible webbing.

4. At each corner on each end of the main fabric straps, fold the clipped point of the seam allowances inward (on a 45° angle), leaving a gap of 1/8" between the end of the interfacing and the folded edge of the seam allowance.

Fold the ends of
seam allowances.

TIP:

Leaving a gap of 1/8" allows for the strap to turn cleanly over the bulk of the turned seam allowances and will create a neat strap end.

5. Fold the seam allowances at the short end of each main fabric strap over the edge of the interfacing, toward the wrong side of the strap. Fuse the turned edges into place, taking care to keep the corners square and straight.

Fold seam allowance
ends over webbing.

TIP:

If you accidentally fuse the seam allowances in the wrong spot, you can carefully peel them back, reposition them, and fuse them down again.

6. On the contrast fabric straps, turn the seam allowances of the long edges over the webbing's backing paper, and press them flat and into place. Snip 3/8" into the seam allowances at the 2" mark from each strap end. This will help the seam allowances to sit flat around the tapered end of the strap. Press the strap very flat to make the creases as sharp as possible.

7. Trim the seam allowance ends, from the crease to 1" down the edge of the seam allowance, and then snip 1/4" into the seam allowance 2" from each end; then adjust the seam allowance a bit to allow the strap end to taper inward.

Fold seam allowances
toward wrong side.

Snip to allow fabric to taper.

8. Remove the backing paper from the webbing on the contrast straps, and fuse all the seam allowances into place on the wrong side of the fabric.

9. Place each main fabric strap, wrong sides together, with a contrast fabric strap, centering the contrast along the length of the main fabric strap. Press to fuse the main and contrast strips together, the full length of each strap. Remember to protect your iron from any exposed fusible webbing with an appliqué mat or baking parchment.

Fuse contrast strap to outer strap.

10. Using a disappearing marker pen or Hera marker on the right side of the main fabric, draw a line across 2" from each end of the strap.

11. Thread your machine with thread to match the main fabric in the needle and thread to match the contrast fabric in the bobbin. On each side of each strap, backstitch neatly at the marker line,

and topstitch 1/16" from the long edge, all the way to the other marker line. Backstitch neatly and pull all thread ends through to the wrong side of the strap.

12. Stitch another row of top stitching along each edge, 1/4" in from the first. You can use a 1/4" foot to do this if it helps.

Topstitch straps.

13. Cut and fuse a rectangle of fusible webbing 1 1/2" × 2" to the wrong (contrast fabric) side of each strap end.

ATTACH THE STRAPS

1. Use a disappearing or Hera marker to mark the strap placements on the bag body. Measure 4" from the top edge and 3" in from each of the side edges. Draw 1" lines to mark the bottom and side edges of the strap placement.

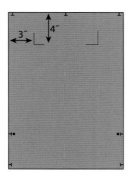

2. Fuse the strap ends in place on the bag body, and use pins to hold the straps securely at the top of the bag body.

3. On each strap end, backstitch neatly over the end of the top stitching and topstitch 1/16" in from the edge, around the bottom end of the strap (attaching it to the bag body). Pivot and topstitch along the mark across the strap.

BASIC BAG

TIP:

When topstitching straps, pivot, reverse, and stitch continuously wherever possible, rather than stopping and starting and backstitching. You'll have fewer loose thread ends to worry about, and the overall effect will be neater.

4. Stitch another row of top stitching around the edge of the strap, 1/4" in from the first, and then stitch another row across the strap, 1/4" above the first.

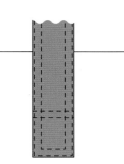

5. Pull all the thread ends through to the wrong side of the fabric and tie them off.

ANCHOR THE STRAPS

This is optional, but if the top of the bag is sagging behind the straps, you can topstitch them through all layers to the facing.

1. Press the straps and facing of the bag, to make sure everything is flat and sitting where it needs to be. Use clips or pins as necessary to hold the strap straight.

2. With thread to match the straps on the upper thread and thread to match the facing in the bobbin, carefully stitch over the top row of top stitching across the top of each strap, through all layers of fabric at the top of the bag. Backstitch neatly and securely at each end.

TIP:

Hold both threads when you begin topstitching, to avoid tangled thread on the facing.

THE IBIZA BUCKET BAG

FINISHED BAG: 12″ × 14″ × 6″

In feminine floral, this drawstring tote is sweet and fun and the perfect casual summer bag. The drawstring elastic top gives extra security to a simple snap closure, and the zippered and compartment pockets on the lining make it easy to carry and access all the essentials. There's ample opportunity for color play with fabrics, and the design works in every style— from shabby chic to urban monotone.

PATTERN PIECES

- Front/Back bag body (pattern piece #1)

- Side panel (pattern piece #2)

- Facing (pattern piece #5)

- Lining (pattern piece #3)

- Lining side panel (pattern piece #4)

- Zipper pocket 2 facing (pattern piece #11)

- Basic bag pocket (pattern piece #23)

- Compartment pocket (pattern piece #8)

- Bag base (pattern piece #6)

- Bag base support (pattern piece #7)

- Straps and casings will be measured and cut according to instructions.

MATERIALS

- 1 yard light decor-weight, sateen, or linen-cotton fabric*

- 7/8 yard medium- or light-weight contrast fabric

- 1 yard light- to medium-weight cotton fabric for lining (quilting weight)

- 2 yards medium-weight fusible woven interfacing

- 1 zipper 8″ to match lining fabric

- 7″ × 13″ Peltex, Timtex, or fast2fuse for bag base support

- 2″ × 11″ nonwoven fusible interfacing (Vilene S320 or Pellon Craft-Fuse) for zipper pocket facing

- 3/4″ magnetic snap

- 2 yards cord elastic (any width)

- 4 plastic cord ends

- 4 O-rings 1″

- 2 cord pulls

- 1/4″ fusible tape

- Hera or disappearing marker

- Gluestick pen (optional)

- Threads to match all fabrics

* I used "Summer Floral" by CurlyPops.

ALTER THE PATTERN

1. Slash and close ¾″ along each horizontal slash line #2 on the following pieces: bag body, lining, bag base, and base support. (See Slash and Close, page 27.)

2. Slash and close ¾″ along each vertical slash line #2 on the following pieces: side panel, lining side panel, and facing.

3. Label the new pattern pieces carefully so that you won't mix them up with the other bag patterns.

4. Use the compartment pocket, zipper pocket 2 facing, and basic bag pocket from the basic bag pattern, without altering them.

Fuse and Cut the Fabric

1. Block fuse interfacing for the bag body, side panel, and facing to the main fabric. Cut 2 of each of these pieces, snip all the notches, and mark all of the dots on the wrong side of the fabric.

2. Cut the bag base in the contrast fabric, and cut the base support in Peltex, Timtex, or fast2fuse.

3. Cut all of the lining, lining side panel, and pocket pieces in lining fabric. Snip all the notches with ⅛″ nicks.

4. For shoulder straps, cut 2 pieces 4″ × 30″ of contrast fabric. Cut 2 interfacing pieces 3″ × 27″. Center the interfacing on the wrong side of each strap, and fuse it securely.

5. For the drawstring casings, cut 2 strips of contrast fabric 2″ × 13½″ and 2 strips 2″ × 5½″.

6. For the O-ring loops, cut a strip of contrast fabric 4″ × 16″.

MAKE THE CASINGS

1. At the short ends of each of the 4 casing pieces, press a ⅜″ turning to the wrong side of fabric.

2. Turn each turned end again, ½″.

3. Unfold each double-turning, and trim the corners of the inner turning, from the fold of fabric to ¾″ down the raw edge.

4. Fold the double-turning again, and stitch it to the outer casing, 1/16″ from the inner folded edge.

5. On the wrong side of each casing piece, fuse ¼″ fusible tape along the long, raw edges. Don't remove the backing paper.

6. Using the backing paper as a folding line, fold the fabric; press the long edges toward the wrong side of fabric.

7. Remove the backing paper.

8. Clip the corners of the turnings from the fold line to ½" down the edge of the turning, and then press to fuse the turning to the back of the casing.

9. On the back of each of the casing pieces, fuse another strip of fusible tape on top of each of the turnings. Remove the backing paper.

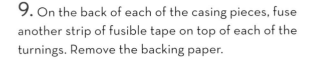

ATTACH THE CASINGS

1. Using a ruler and Hera or disappearing marker, measure and mark a line 3" from the top of each of the bag body and side panel pieces.

2. Matching the top edging of each casing to the line on each bag piece, center the casing pieces horizontally, and press to fuse them.

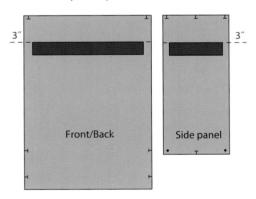

Front/Back   Side panel

3. Along both long edges on each casing, neatly topstitch as close to the folded edge as you can, pivot, and sew 2 or 3 stitches.

4. Stitch a second row, ⅛" in from the first. Backstitch neatly and pull all threads through to the wrong side of the fabric.

MAKE THE BAG BASE

Follow the instructions in External Textile Bag Base (page 53).

CONSTRUCT THE BAG BODY

Follow the instructions in Basic Bag (page 66) to assemble the bag body and make the facing, taking particular care to remove the interfacing from the side seam allowances wherever possible.

Do not attach the facing yet.

MAKE THE STRAPS

Make the O-Ring Loops

1. Follow the instructions for the four-fold strap (page 45) to make a long, narrow strap with the 4″ × 16″ fabric strip.

NOTE:

This is a longer strap than you actually need, so you can trim off scruffy ends and pick the best bits of your top stitching to use on the straps.

2. Trim off the raw ends, and cut the strap into 4 pieces 3½″ long.

3. Fold each length through a 1″ O-ring, and stitch the ends of the strap together, ¼″ from the raw edges.

Construct the Shoulder Straps

1. Use the basic bagged-out method (page 46) to make 2 straps, following the steps to make straps with rings at both ends.

2. Turn the straps through the O-rings 2″ from each end, and stitch the ends to the main strap (page 48).

Attach the Straps

1. At the top edge of the bag, measure 1″ in (toward CF/CB) from each of the side seams, and make a small mark or snip on the seam allowance.

2. Align the outer edge of each strap end with a notch, and place the straps right side down on the right side of fabric. Check that there are no twists in the straps, line up the raw ends of the strap with the top edge of the bag, and stitch the strap ends into place, ¼″ from the top edge of the bag.

ATTACH THE FACING

Follow the instructions in Basic Bag (page 71) to make, attach, understitch, and topstitch the facing around the top of the bag.

INSERT THE MAGNETIC SNAP

Follow the instructions in Basic Bag-Making Techniques (page 58) to attach the magnetic snap.

ADD POCKETS TO THE LINING

1. Follow the instructions in Compartment Pocket (page 30) to add the pocket to one lining piece.

2. Follow the instructions in Exposed Zipper Pocket (page 36) for the other lining piece.

SEW, ATTACH, AND FINISH THE LINING

Follow the instructions in Basic Bag (page 74) to construct, attach, and finish the lining.

THREAD ELASTIC THROUGH THE CASINGS

1. Cut the elastic cord in half, and attach a bodkin or large safety pin to one long end.

2. Beginning at one corner of the bag, thread the elastic through all the casings around the bag. Pull both ends of the elastic so that at least 4" of each end is visible outside the casing.

3. Thread a cord pull over both of the ends, and pull it up toward the casings on the bag.

4. Thread a plastic cord end over each end of the elastic. Tie several knots—one over the top of the other—to make a big knot at each end of the elastic cord, and then pull the cord end over the top of the knot.

5. Starting at a diagonally opposite corner on the bag, thread the other piece of elastic cord through the casings. Pull both ends of the cord out at least 4", and attach the cord pull and cord ends as in Steps 3 and 4.

6. Pull the cord ends through the cord pull until about 6" of each end is dangling below, and even out the gathers around the top of the bag.

THE OSAKA PLEATED HANDBAG

FINISHED BAG: 12½" × 9½" × 6"

This is a sweet and simple bag with loads of feminine charm. It's a small but surprisingly roomy handbag. The sewing is uncomplicated, but the details are sharp, with structured straps and base and topstitched pleats and seams. The weighted strap adds extra strength and security to the magnetic snap closure. On this uncomplicated design, you will need to alter all the pieces of the bag. This will help you to understand how altering the proportions of a bag will affect the individual pattern pieces, and will prepare you for more detailed alterations.

PATTERN PIECES

- Front/Back bag body (pattern piece #1)
- Side panel (pattern piece #2)
- Facing (pattern piece #5)
- Lining (pattern piece #3)
- Lining side panel (pattern piece #4)
- Zipper pocket 2 facing (pattern piece #11)
- Patch pocket (pattern piece #22)
- Bag base (pattern piece #6)
- Bag base support (pattern piece #7)
- Straps and zipper pocket lining will be cut according to instructions.

MATERIALS

- 1⅛ yards quilting-weight fabric for outer bag*
- ½ yards quilting-weight fabric for lining
- 1¾ yards medium-weight woven interfacing (Shape-Flex or heavier)
- 1¾ yards medium-light woven interfacing
- 7" × 13" pelmet interfacing (Vilene S520 or Pellon 520F Deco-Fuse) for bag base support
- 3" × 12" nonwoven fusible interfacing (Vilene S320 or Pellon Craft-Fuse) for zipper pocket lining

- 1¼ yard of ½" (12mm) polyester boning
- 1 zipper 6" to match the lining fabric
- 1 O-ring 1½"
- 1 magnetic snap ¾"
- 1 sheet of template plastic
- 6 purse feet ½"
- ¼" fusible tape
- Fabric gluestick
- Quilt-basting spray
- Threads to match all fabrics

I used "Flutter" by Riley Blake.

ALTER THE PATTERN

NOTE:

If you have already made the Ibiza Bucket Bag (page 80), you can use the facing, bag base, and bag base support pieces that you slashed and closed for that project, and simply make the adjustment on the horizontal slash line on the side panel and lining side panel pieces.

1. Slash and close 4½" on horizontal slash line #1 on each of the following pieces: bag body, lining, side panel, and lining side panel (see Slash and Close, page 27).

2. Slash and close ¾" on horizontal slash line #2 on each of the following pattern pieces: bag body, lining, bag base, and bag base support.

3. Slash and close ¾" on each vertical slash line #2 on the following pattern pieces: side panel, lining side panel, and facing.

4. Label the new pattern pieces carefully so that you won't mix them up with the other bag patterns.

FUSE AND CUT THE FABRIC

1. Block fuse medium-weight interfacing, and cut 2 each of the bag body, side panel, and facing pieces from the main fabric.

NOTE:

When working with heavier interfacings, I prefer to block fuse rather than cut the interfacing without seam allowances, even when it will have to be removed from the seam allowances during the sewing process. That way, I only need to cut once—through fabric and interfacing. Also, with the amount of heat and pressure needed to fuse the interfacing correctly, it's easiest to use an ironing press (if you have one), rather than a domestic iron, and any shrinkage or distortion in the fabric or interfacing will happen before cutting, making cutting more accurate.

If you are uncomfortable with this method, feel free to cut all your interfacing pieces individually and without seam allowances, and press them to the wrong side of fabric.

2. On the top edge of each bag body piece, measure 3" in from each side, and snip a small notch. Measure ½" in from each notch (toward the center of the bag piece), and snip another notch. These are the handle placement notches.

3. Block fuse light interfacing to the lining fabric (or cut interfacing without seam allowances) and cut the lining and lining side panel pieces.

4. Cut 1 zipper pocket 2 facing (pattern piece #11) in lining and in interfacing (see Exposed Zipper Pocket, page 36). Don't fuse the interfacing to the fabric yet.

5. Cut a pocket lining for the exposed zipper pocket 8½″ × 10″ in lining fabric. Cut 1 patch pocket in lining fabric.

6. Cut 1 bag base in the main (or contrast) fabric. Cut the bag base support in pelmet interfacing (Vilene S520 or Pellon 520F Deco-Fuse) and in template plastic.

7. Cut 2 straps 2⅜″ × 22″ from the main fabric. Cut 2 lengths of ½″ polyester boning, 22″ each.

8. Cut 1 strap 4″ × 10″ from the main (or contrast) fabric for the closure weight. Cut a 1½″ × 10″ strip of light interfacing and fuse it, centered, to the wrong side of the strap fabric.

TIP:

If the polyester boning has been stored in a tight roll, it might have too much curl in it. You can lightly iron it flat.

MAKE AND ATTACH THE BAG BASE

1. On the pelmet interfacing, mark the purse feet positions 1″ from the long edges of the base, 1½″ from each of the short ends, and in the center of the long horizontal placement lines.

2. Follow the instructions to make Structured External Bag Base with Purse Feet (page 55).

NOTE:

If you prefer an easier route, you could make the internal textile base (see Internal [Textile] Bag Base, page 52). The effect will not be quite as sharp and structured, but it will be easier to manipulate the fabric around the sewing machine. If you are new to sewing, try the internal base first.

CONSTRUCT THE BAG BODY

Follow the instructions in Basic Bag (page 66) to assemble the bag body, taking particular care to remove interfacing from every side seam. Press the side seam allowances open (without topstitching).

STRAPS

Prepare the Straps

1. Follow the instructions to press the straps in preparation for a four-fold strap (page 45).

2. Open up the folds and slide a length of polyester boning into one of the outer folds.

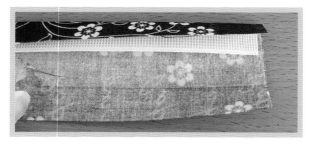

TIP:

Quilt-basting spray or a 1"-wide strip of double-sided fusible webbing will help hold the boning in place until it is stitched. Quilt-basting spray also can hold the layers of the strap together when you fold it for stitching.

3. Fold the strap back together, ready for stitching, and give it another press.

4. Topstitch both four-fold straps 1/16" from each edge, with the boning sandwiched between. (You can sew straight through boning with a normal sewing machine.) Stitch another row of top stitching, centered between the 2 outer rows.

5. Trim the straps to remove any scruffy ends and to shorten each handle to 21".

ATTACH THE HANDLES

1. Place a handle on the right side of a bag piece, with one raw end of the strap aligned with the top of the bag. Match the side of the handle with the 2 folded edges to the outer notch and the single folded edge to the inner notch.

2. Stitch the handle in place within the 1/2" seam allowance at the top edge of the bag piece. Curl the handle around, without twisting, and match the other end to the notches on the other side of the bag piece. Stitch the handle ends into place, taking care to keep the first few inches of handle at a right angle to the top edge of the bag.

3. Repeat Steps 1 and 2 for the other handle.

MAKE THE CLOSURE WEIGHT

1. Follow the instructions for a bagged-out strap without rings (page 46) using the 4" × 10" piece cut earlier. Topstitch 3/8" in from each of the side edges, and then topstitch 2 more rows, spaced evenly between.

2. Thread the strap through the 1½" O-ring, and fold it to match the short, raw ends (with the right side of the strap facing outward).

3. Draw a Hera or disappearing marker line across the strap, 1" from the folded end.

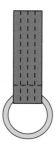

4. Pin, glue, or fuse the 2 ends of the strap together between the marker line and the raw ends.

5. Beginning at the raw edge, topstitch the straps together 1/16″ from the side edge to the marker line. Pivot and stitch across the marker line, and then pivot and stitch the other side edge, the same as the first.

6. With right sides of the fabric facing, center the raw ends of the closure weight strap over the center-back notch of the bag. Stitch the strap to the top edge of the bag 1/4″ from the top edge.

MAKE AND ATTACH THE FACING

1. Follow the instructions in Basic Bag (page 71) to make the facing.

2. Attach the facing to the bag (page 72); keep the last few inches of handle at a right angle to the top of the bag.

3. Before edgestitching and topstitching, remove interfacing from the seam allowances at the top edge of the bag and facing.

4. Topstitch around the top of the bag, a scant 3/8″ from the edge. Again, keep the handles at a right angle as you secure their ends in the top-stitched edge of the bag.

INSERT THE MAGNETIC SNAP

Follow the instructions (page 58) to insert a magnetic snap in the facing.

MAKE THE LINING

1. Follow the instructions (page 28) to add the patch pocket to one of the lining pieces.

2. Follow the instructions (page 36) to add the exposed zipper pocket to the other lining piece.

3. Follow the instructions in Basic Bag (page 74) to construct the lining, taking extra care to remove the interfacing from the seam allowances, clip all the corners of the seam allowances, and press all the seam allowances open. The reduction of bulk in the seams is very important here.

ATTACH THE LINING

1. Follow the instructions (page 75) to attach the lining to the facing.

2. Slipstitch (ladder stitch) to close the gap in the base seam of the lining.

TOPSTITCH THE SIDE SEAMS

Press and Pin

1. Working on the end of the ironing board or on a sleeve board, press a side seam, aligning and flattening the bag and lining seams together.

2. Hold the lining in place on the inside as you fold the bag along the seamline, so that the lining will be caught in the middle of the fold. Press the fold to crease it sharply, and pin (with the pins at right angles to the edge of the bag) to hold the fold in this position.

3. Repeat Steps 1 and 2 to press and pin the other 3 side seams.

4. Holding the threads as you begin to sew, backstitch neatly and topstitch each folded seam, a generous ¼" (or scant ⅜") from the edge. As you near the base of the bag, slow down and maneuver the bag base to allow you to sew as close as you can to the end of the side seam.

5. Somewhere within the last 1" of seam (before you reach the base), it will become too awkward to continue sewing parallel to the folded seam edge. At this point, pivot and stitch toward the folded edge, as close to the bottom corner as you can manage. Backstitch neatly on the folded edge of the seam.

STITCH THE TUCKS

1. On the top edge of the bag, measure ½″ in from the inside edge of each handle. Fold the top 2½″ of the bag in a vertical line (outside of bag on the outside, with the facing caught inside the fold) from each of these points. Press and pin to hold the tucks in place.

4. Topstitch the tuck through all layers of fabric, ³⁄₈″ from the folded seam on the facing.

2. Hold your threads to start stitching, and backstitch neatly on the top edge of the bag; then topstitch each of the tucks ³⁄₈″ from the folded edge. Backtack neatly at the end of each row of top stitching.

You've finished your handbag!

3. On the center of each side panel, fold the tucks toward the inside of the bag, pinching the fold along the side seam of the facing, with the outside of the side panel caught in the fold of fabric.

THE MARRAKESH OVERNIGHTER

FINISHED BAG: 16½" × 14" × 7½"

This fashionably large, unstructured carryall is perfect for overnight stays, shopping, family outings, and any time you have to carry more than the everyday essentials. This project will ease you into making more detailed straps and handles. Other design details are kept to a minimum, and you can focus on developing turned-edge techniques to make straps and handles that look like those on the fanciest leather bags. Use large-scale prints on decor-weight fabric to make a stunning statement bag or a solid color for understated glamour.

PATTERN PIECES

- Front/Back bag body (pattern piece #1)
- Side panel (pattern piece #2)
- Facing (pattern piece #5)
- Lining (pattern piece #3)
- Lining side panel (pattern piece #4)
- Zipper pocket 1 facing (pattern piece #9)
- Basic bag pocket (pattern piece #23)
- Compartment pocket (pattern piece #8)
- Bag base (pattern piece #6)
- Bag base support (pattern piece #7)
- Straps will be measured and cut according to instructions.

NOTE:

The pattern is written to include a zippered pocket and a compartment pocket in the lining, but you can choose to include any of the pockets in this design.

MATERIALS

- 1½ yards decor-weight fabric*
- 1⅓ yards cotton drill/gabardine in contrast color (You will have a lot left over, but you need the length for the shoulder strap.)
- ¼ yard light cotton (in a color to match your straps)
- 1⅓ yards quilting-weight fabric for lining
- 2¼ yards fusible medium-weight interfacing
- 8" × 17" pelmet interfacing (Vilene S520 or Pellon 520F Deco-Fuse)

(continued on page 96)

Materials, continued

- 2″ × 11″ nonwoven fusible interfacing (Vilene S320 or Pellon Craft-Fuse) for zipper pocket lining

- 16″ × 26″ fusible webbing

- 1 sheet of template plastic

- 6 purse feet ½″

- 1 slide adjuster 1″

- 2 O-rings 1″

- 4 O-rings 1¼″ or 1½″

- 1″ bias tape maker

- 1 zipper 8″ to match lining fabric

- ¼″ fusible tape

- ¾″ magnetic snap

- Fabric gluestick

- Quilt-basting spray

- Saddler's punch

- Hera or disappearing marker

- Threads to match all fabrics

I used "Dipped Dots" by Kristen Doran.

ALTER THE PATTERN

1. Slash and open 4″ along each vertical slash line #1 on the following pieces: bag body, lining, facing, compartment pocket, bag base, and bag base support. (See Slash and Open, page 26)

2. Label the new pattern pieces carefully so that you won't mix them up with the other bag patterns.

3. Use the side panel (pattern piece #2), lining side panel (pattern piece #4), and zipper pocket (pattern pieces #11 and #23) from the basic bag pattern.

Fuse and Cut the Fabric

1. Block fuse interfacing (page 20) to the main fabric for the bag body, facing, and side panel. Cut 2 of each of these pieces, snip all the notches, and mark all of the dots on the wrong side of fabric.

2. Cut the bag base in the contrast fabric. Cut the base support in pelmet interfacing (Vilene S520 or Pellon 520F Deco-Fuse) and also in template plastic.

3. Cut the lining, lining side panel, and pocket pieces in lining fabric. Snip all the notches with ⅛″ nicks.

FOLDED STRAP HANDLES

These handles take a bit more work, but the results look very professional. The technique is based on one that is used for leather, but it's adapted to take fraying edges of fabric into account. I recommend doing a test strap with this method first. If your machine is not capable, or if you're daunted by this technique, you can substitute four-fold straps with rings (page 45) for these handles.

What is most important here is accurate measurement and cutting straight lines. The interfacing and the backing paper of the fusible webbing are used throughout the process as folding lines and as a means of keeping everything aligned squarely. Therefore, use a quilting ruler and rotary cutter (not scissors), and take care to measure and align everything accurately before fusing anything into place.

Prepare the Outer Strap

1. Cut 2 straps from the cotton drill fabric 3½″ × 26″.

2. Cut 2 interfacing strips 2″ × 18″.

3. Cut paper-backed fusible webbing 2″ × 26″. Draw a line 4″ in from each short end.

4. On each short end of the webbing, measure and mark ¼″ in from the sides. Draw a diagonal line between the 4″ line on the long edges and the ¼″ mark on the short ends. Cut along the diagonal lines to taper the ends of the webbing as shown.

TIP:

Instead of drawing the line, simply use a rotary cutter and ruler to cut between the 2 marked points on the webbing. You can cut 2 layers at a time.

5. Center an interfacing strip on each of the strap pieces, on the wrong side of fabric. There should be 4″ of strap on each short end and an even ¾″ seam allowance along each of the long edges. Fuse it into place.

6. Fuse the fusible webbing over the top of the interfacing, with the tapered ends of the webbing extending to the short ends of the strap. Leave the backing paper on.

7. Using the backing paper of the fusible webbing as a fold line, turn and press the seam allowances over the top of the webbing and interfacing. Press the strap flat to make the creases as sharp as possible. Snip ³⁄₈″ into the seam allowances at the 4″ mark from each strap end. This will help the seam allowances sit flat around the tapered end of the strap.

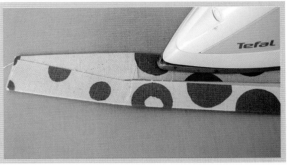

8. On the tapered ends of each strap, trim the seam allowances from the end of the crease to about 2″ in from each short end. Then trim the rest of the seam allowance to an even ¾″.

9. Peel the backing paper off the fusible webbing and, placing the straps webbing-side down on an appliqué mat or baking paper, press them to stick all of the seam allowances into place.

Prepare the Inner Strap

1. Cut 2 lengths of light cotton fabric (in a color to match your straps) 3″ × 24″.

2. Fold and press the fabric as if to make 2 four-fold straps, but then open the center fold and press each strap flat, with the raw edges of fabric at the center on the underside. We'll now call them inner straps.

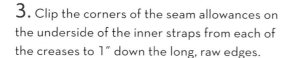

3. Clip the corners of the seam allowances on the underside of the inner straps from each of the creases to 1″ down the long, raw edges.

4. Spray the underside of the inner straps with quilt-basting spray (or cut 2 strips of fusible webbing 1½″ × 24″ and fuse one to the back of each of the inner straps), completely covering the raw edges of fabric.

5. Center an inner strap horizontally and vertically on the wrong side of each outer strap, and fuse it into place. There will be 1″ of outer strap extending beyond each end of the inner strap.

Construct the Strap

1. Using a Hera or disappearing fabric marker, draw a line across the strap on the right side of fabric, 5″ from each short end. Draw another line at the 5¼″ mark.

2. From the raw edge on each end of each strap, topstitch ⅟₁₆″ from the folded side edge to the 5¼″ line. Pivot and stitch a generous ¼″, then pivot and topstitch parallel to the first row of stitches, back to the raw edge. The stitches should catch the inner strap to the back of the strap. Repeat on the other edge of the strap.

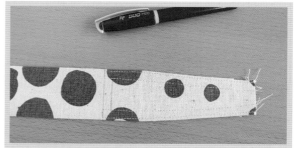

3. Push each tapered strap end through a bag ring, and fold the end (inner sides together) to align the end of the inner strap to the 5″ line, with the bag ring sitting in the fold. The raw end of the strap will extend past the 5″ mark by 1″. Pin, glue, or fuse the end of the strap into place.

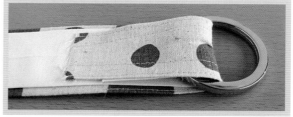

4. At both ends of each strap, topstitch (from the right side of the strap) along the 5¼" line, backstitching at each end of the stitch line. Pull all the excess threads through to the wrong side of fabric.

5. Cut another 2 strips of fusible webbing 2" × 15", and center each over the inner side of a strap. Fuse the webbing and remove the backing paper.

6. Fold each strap in half lengthwise, and press to fuse it together. You may need to pin or bulldog clip the ends near the rings, to stop them from opening up again.

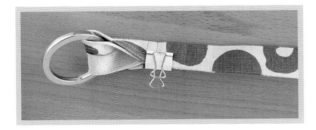

7. Beginning halfway along the 5" line (and holding the threads securely), backstitch neatly and then stitch toward the twice-folded edge side of the strap.

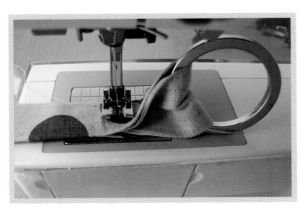

8. Pivot and stitch the long folded edges together, 1/16" in from the edge (or as close to it as you can). Pivot and stitch across the 5" line on the other side, and then stitch 1/16" in from the long, single-folded edge. Pivot and stitch back onto the first 5" line.

9. In a continuous line (using reverse stitching or stitching over short lines of stitching), topstitch 2 more rows along the length of each strap, spaced roughly ¼" apart.

NOTE:

By stitching in a continuous line, you will reduce the need to stop, start, and backstitch as you stitch all the rows of top stitching, and you won't have as many ends of thread to tidy up later.

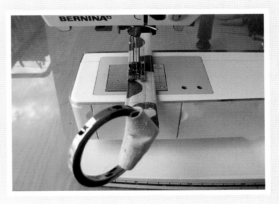

THE O-RING TABS

These tabs stitch onto the body of the bag and are a design feature that makes a simple bag a stylish one. They take a little bit of extra work, but the results are worth the trouble.

If you prefer to keep things simple, you can attach these handles with four-fold straps (page 45) stitched into the top of the bag (like the shoulder strap, page 84).

Prepare the O-Ring Tabs

1. Cut 4 strips of medium-weight fusible woven interfacing 1½" × 6". Cut 4 strips of paper-backed fusible webbing 1½" × 6¾".

2. On each of the interfacing strips, measure and draw a line 2" from one end. Measure ¼" in from either side of the end of the strip. Draw a diagonal line between each ¼" and its corresponding 2" mark (on the same side edge). Cut along this line to taper the end of the strip.

TIP:

Layer several strips together and trim them with a ruler and rotary cutter to cut the tapered ends.

3. Repeat Step 2 to taper the ends of each of the webbing strips.

4. Aligning the long edges of the strips with the straight grain of fabric, fuse the interfacing strips to the wrong side of the contrast fabric, leaving a clear 1½" of fabric between each strip and a clear 1" below the square end.

5. Using a rotary cutter and ruler, measure and cut a ¾" seam allowance around each of the interfacing strips on all sides except the tapered end.

6. Cut a 2" × 25" strip of light fabric, and run it through a 1" bias tape maker to turn the edges under. *Otherwise,* follow instructions to make a four-fold strap (page 45) to the point where the 2 outer edges are folded to the center.

Construct the O-Ring Tabs

1. Center and fuse the webbing into place (over the interfacing) on the wrong side of each fabric strip (O-ring tab). Do not remove the backing paper.

2. Snip ⅜" into the seam allowance at the 2" mark on each O-ring tab. This will allow the seam allowance to fold around the tapered end and sit flat.

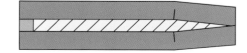

3. Use the edge of the backing paper and interfacing as a fold line to turn and press the seam allowances to the interfacing side. Press the turnings flat.

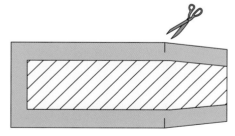

4. Trim the corners of the turnings from the end of each crease to 1″ down each long seam allowance edge.

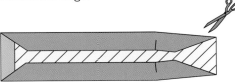

5. Remove the backing paper and, turning the webbing side onto an appliqué mat or baking paper, press the turnings into place.

6. On the square ends of each O-ring tab, fold the corners of the seam allowance in at a 45° angle, toward the wrong side of fabric, leaving ⅛″ clear between the short end of the interfacing and the folded corner fabric.

Leave a gap.

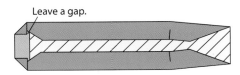

7. Fold the seam allowance at the square end of each tab to the wrong side of fabric, using the edge of the interfacing as a fold line; press to fuse the turning into place.

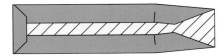

8. Cut the strip of light fabric binding from Step 6 of Prepare the O-Ring Tabs (page 100) into 4 lengths, each measuring 5″. Using basting spray, fabric glue, or webbing, stick one length of binding to the wrong side of each tab, beginning where the square end turning finishes and ending about ½″ short of the tapered end.

9. On the right side of each O-ring tab, measure and draw a line (with a Hera or disappearing marker) 2″ from the square end. Draw a second line 1¾″ in from the same end.

10. On each O-ring tab, between the tapered end and the 2″ mark, topstitch 1/16″ in from each folded edge. Pivot and turn to stitch a second row on each edge, ¼″ in from the first.

1¾″ 2″

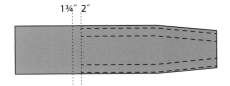

Attach the O-Ring Tabs to the Handles

1. With the right side of fabric facing outward, thread the tapered end of an O-ring tab through each of the O-rings attached to the handles. Fold the tapered ends to the back of each tab, with the O-rings in the fold.

2. Match the raw tapered end of the tab to the end of the binding (near the square end). Pin, glue, or fuse the tapered end to the back of the tab, keeping any adhesives within the 2″ area at the square ends.

3. From the right side of fabric, topstitch across each of the 2″ marker lines.

4. Cut 4 pieces of fusible webbing 1½″ × 2″, and fuse each to the square end of an O-ring tab.

Attach the Handles

1. On both front and back bag body pieces, measure and draw a Hera or disappearing marker line 4″ in from each of the side edges, from the top edge of the bag piece to 4″ below. Draw a line 4″ below the top edge of the bag, between the 2 vertical lines.

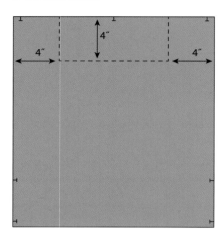

2. Match the bottom edge of each tab to the corner of the marker lines, and pin the tabs into place. Press from the inside of the bag to fuse the tabs to the fabric of the bag, and remove the pins.

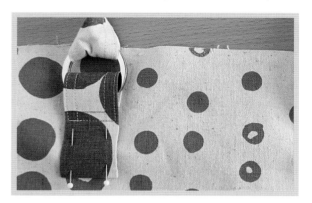

3. Topstitch the tabs to the bag 1/16″ from the edge, from the 2″ marker line to the bottom of the tab, across the square end and back to the 2″ line. Pivot and turn to stitch a second row, 1/4″ in from the first, around the square end of the tab and then back across the 1 3/4″ marker line. Backstitch neatly and pull all the threads through to the wrong side of fabric.

MAKE THE BAG BASE

1. On the pelmet interfacing, mark the purse feet positions 1 1/2″ from the long edges of the base, 2″ in from each of the short ends, and in the center of the long horizontal placement lines.

2. Follow the instructions in Structured External Bag Base with Purse Feet (page 55).

CONSTRUCT THE BAG BODY

1. Follow the instructions in Basic Bag (page 66) to assemble the bag body.

2. Do not attach the facing yet.

THE ADJUSTABLE SHOULDER STRAP

Make the O-Ring Loops

1. Cut a strap 4″ × 8″ in contrast fabric, and follow the basic four-fold strap method (page 45) to fold and topstitch it.

2. Cut the strap into 2 pieces each 3″ long, and fold each length through a 1″ O-ring.

3. With the O-ring in the fold, stitch the raw ends on each strap together (to make loops) 1/4″ from the raw ends.

Make the Shoulder Strap

1. Cut a strap 4″ × 48″ (or longer if you wish) in contrast fabric.

2. Cut and fuse interfacing to the width and length of the strap, except the last 1¼″ on each end.

3. Follow the instructions for the four-fold strap with a ring at each end (page 45). Remember to trim out the excess fabric at each end of the strap before topstitching all the layers together.

4. Follow the instructions for an adjustable strap (page 50) to attach the slide adjuster and O-rings.

Attach the Shoulder Strap

1. With the right side of the shoulder strap facing the right side of the bag, match the raw ends of an O-ring loop to the center notch on the top of each side panel.

2. Stitch the O-ring loops into place, ¼″ from the top edge.

THE FACING

Follow the instructions in Basic Bag (page 71) to make, attach, understitch, and topstitch the facing around the top of the bag.

ATTACH THE MAGNETIC SNAP

Follow the instructions in Basic Bag-Making Techniques to attach the magnetic snap (page 58).

ADD POCKETS TO THE LINING

1. Follow the instructions (page 30) to add the compartment pocket to one or both of the lining pieces.

2. Follow the instructions (page 31) to attach the basic zippered pocket to one of the lining pieces.

SEW, ATTACH, AND FINISH THE LINING

Follow the instructions in Basic Bag (page 74) to construct, attach, and finish the lining.

THE AVIGNON TRAVELER

FINISHED BAG: 16½" × 14½" × 7½"

This roomy, multipocketed bag has a feature panel on both sides (to show off your favorite fabric) and lots of modern, casual style. The methods in this project are simple, but the results are professional and rewarding. You'll learn a simple overhanging zippered closure and an alternative strap placement. The base is structured and includes purse feet, making it a practical, hardwearing travel bag or everyday carryall.

PATTERN PIECES

- Side panel (pattern piece #2)
- Facing (pattern piece #5)
- Lining (pattern piece #3)
- Lining side panel (pattern piece #4)
- Zipper pocket 2 facing (pattern piece #11)
- Basic bag pocket (pattern piece #23)
- Compartment pocket (pattern piece #8)
- Bag base (pattern piece #6)
- Bag base support (pattern piece #7)
- Straps and other components will be measured and cut according to instructions.

MATERIALS

- ⅝ yard decor-weight feature fabric*
- 1¼ yards light denim or drill, in base color to match the feature panel.
- 1⅓ yards lining fabric
- 2¾ yards medium-weight fusible woven interfacing
- 8" × 17" pelmet interfacing (Vilene S520 or Pellon 520F Deco-Fuse)
- 3" × 12" nonwoven fusible interfacing (Vilene S320 or Pellon Craft-Fuse) for zipper pocket lining

- 1 sheet template plastic
- 6 purse feet ½"
- 4 O-rings 1¼"
- 2" × 12" fusible webbing
- 1" bias tape maker
- 2 zippers 16" to match outer fabrics
- 1 jacket zipper 26" (or 28") to match the main fabric
- 1 zipper 8" to match lining fabric
- ¼" fusible tape
- Fabric gluestick
- Saddler's punch
- Threads to match all fabrics

I used "Grevillea" by Ink & Spindle.

NOTE:

This pattern is written to include 2 zipper pockets on the outside of the bag. You can choose to include any, all, or none of the lining pockets in this design.

ALTER THE PATTERN

1. Slash and open 4″ along each vertical slash line #1 on the following pieces: lining, facing, compartment pocket, bag base, and bag base support. *For this design, you'll use the front/back lining pattern for the outer bag body as well as for the lining.* (See Slash and Open, page 26.)

2. To make the top center panel of the bag, trace the facing pattern onto another piece of paper, and then use the altered lining pattern to measure the width of the panel. Align the CF/CB notches, and trim away the excess width on either side of the traced facing pattern.

3. Label the new pattern pieces carefully so that you won't mix them up with the other bag patterns.

4. Use the side panel, lining side panel, and pocket pattern pieces from the basic bag pattern.

FUSE AND CUT THE FABRIC

1. Using the lining pattern piece, block fuse interfacing and cut the bag body (front and back) from the feature fabric.

2. Block fuse interfacing and cut the facing and side panels in the main (base color) fabric. Also block fuse and cut the new top center panel pieces. On each piece, snip all the notches and mark all of the dots on the wrong side of fabric.

3. Cut the bag base in the main fabric. Cut the base support in pelmet interfacing (Vilene S520 or Pellon 520F Deco-Fuse) and also in template plastic.

4. Cut pocket linings for the external pockets (behind the feature center panels), 17″ × 23″.

5. Cut 2 lining, lining side panel, and pocket pieces in lining fabric.

EXTERNAL ZIPPER POCKETS

The Zippered Front Pockets

1. Lay the zipper facedown on the right side of the bag body (feature fabric), lining up the edge of the zipper tape and the top edge of the fabric piece. Take care to position the zipper so that the metal stoppers at the end of the zipper will not be caught in any of the side seams.

2. Open the zipper and begin to stitch the zipper tape to the bag body, ¼″ from the edge. When you've sewn 3″–4″, lower the needle, raise the presser foot, and close the zipper to move the zipper head out of the way.

TIP:

Match the thread in the needle to the outer fabric and the bobbin thread to the lining fabric.

3. Take the pocket lining and, matching a 17″ side to the zipper edge, place the pocket lining and bag body right sides together. The zipper will be sandwiched between.

4. Align the edges and sew the lining into place, following the first line of stitching that attached the zipper to the bag body. Remember to move the zipper head out of the way as you sew past it.

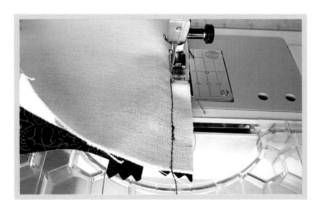

TIP:

It's important that the pocket lining does not stretch or pucker as it is sewn to the outer bag and zipper. You can use pins, fusible tape, or fabric gluestick to hold the lining in place if necessary (whichever method is most comfortable for you).

5. Hold onto the zipper, and turn both the lining and fabric to the right side. Press both the bag body and the lining back from the zipper.

6. Topstitch ¹⁄₁₆″ from the edge of the seam to hold the outer and lining fabrics together. Then, stitch another row of top stitching ¼″ from the first.

7. Place the top center panel right side down over the right side of the zipper and bag body piece. Match the bottom edge of the top center panel to the top edge of the zipper tape, and align the short side edges with the side edges of the bag body piece.

8. Stitch the zipper to the top center panel with a ¼" seam allowance, moving the zipper head out of the way as necessary. Take care to keep the panel in alignment with the bottom panel. Don't let it stretch or pucker as you stitch it.

9. Without moving the top center panel, fold the pocket lining (right sides of fabric together) to match the other 17" edge of the pocket to the back of the zipper. Stitch it in place along the edge of the zipper with a ¼" seam allowance. Press to crease the fold in the bottom of the pocket lining.

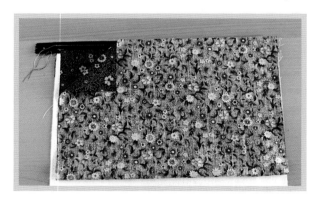

10. Fold the top center panel upward so that you can see the right side of the fabric and the zipper. Fold all the seam allowances toward the top. Press the top center panel flat, over the seam allowances.

11. Change the upper thread to match the top center panel, and topstitch ¹⁄₁₆" from the edge of the seam to hold the panel to all layers of zipper and seam allowances. If you choose, you can also stitch another row, ¼" from the first.

12. Stitch the side edges of the pocket lining to the bag body, ³⁄₈" from the side edges of the bag body.

13. Repeat Steps 1–12 to construct the pocket on the other side of the bag.

THE STRAPS

Cut the Straps

1. Cut 2 side panel straps 4" × 13" in main fabric (no interfacing).

2. Cut 2 shoulder straps 4" × 39". Cut interfacing for the straps 3¼" × 36".

TIP:

The interfacing is cut just wide enough to be caught in the seam of the strap without extending too far onto the seam allowances. With such long, narrow straps, it would be easy for the interfacing to come loose during turning, and stitching it into the seam will prevent this from happening.

Make the Shoulder Straps

1. Center the interfacing on the wrong side of each shoulder strap piece, and fuse it into place.

2. Follow the instructions for a bagged-out strap with rings at both ends (page 46) to make the shoulder straps.

Make the Side Panel Straps

1. Fold each of the straps, right sides together, to match the 2 long edges.

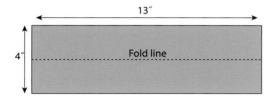

2. Stitch the long edges together with a ½" seam allowance, backstitching each end of each seam.

3. Clip the corners of the seam allowance to 1", and press the seam open.

4. Turn the straps through to the right side, and press them flat, with the seam in the center.

5. From the right side of the strap (the side without the seam), topstitch ¼" in from each of the folded edges, and then stitch 3 more rows, evenly spaced, between the outer rows of top stitching.

6. Fold and press a crease across each strap end, 2" from each end toward the wrong (seamed) side of the strap.

7. Thread an O-ring over each end of each strap. Fold the straps along the crease (2" from the end), and pin the ends in place to make loops around each O-ring.

Attach the Side Panel Straps

1. Cut 2 strips of fusible webbing 1¼" × 6". Center and fuse one on the wrong side of the side panel straps.

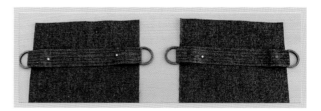

2. On the right side of fabric on each of the side panel pieces, measure and draw a Hera or disappearing marker line, 4" below (and parallel to) the top edge.

3. Remove the backing paper from the fusible webbing, and place a strap (right side up) on each of the side panels. Center each strap horizontally, with the bottom edge of the strap on the marker line. Cover the strap with a pressing cloth, and use steam to fuse it into place.

4. Using a Hera or disappearing marker, draw a line 1½″ from the folded edge on each strap end. Draw another line 1⅞″ from each folded end.

5. Using a tailor's awl to poke in any raw edges of fabric at the ends of the straps, stitch the straps into place 1⁄16″ from the long edges, and stitch in a rectangle shape over the 2 short lines at each end (stitching twice over each 1½″ line).

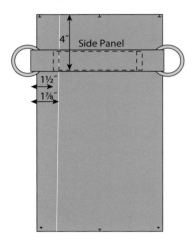

MAKE THE BAG BASE

NOTE:

If zippers are a big challenge for you, you may want to simplify the rest of the design to make it a less daunting project. You can do this by swapping the structured external base for an internal textile base (page 52). This will make a softer, slouchier bag shape, which will be more easily managed around the sewing machine as you construct the bag.

1. On the pelmet interfacing, mark the purse feet positions 1½″ from the long edges of the base, 2″ in from each of the short ends, and in the center of the long horizontal placement lines.

2. Follow the instructions in Structured External Bag Base with Purse Feet (page 55).

CONSTRUCT THE BAG BODY

1. Follow the instructions in Basic Bag (page 66) to assemble the bag body, but instead of turning the side seam allowances to the center, turn them toward the side panels and edgestitch the side panel side of the seam.

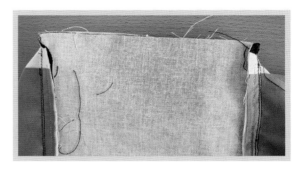

2. Draw another line across each side panel strap, 1⅛″ from the folded edge; then use this line as a stitch guide to topstitch another row, through all layers of the bag fabric and seam allowances. Pivot and stitch another rectangle-shaped reinforcement on the strap. You may also stitch an X in the center of this rectangle. Backstitch and pull all threads to the wrong side of fabric.

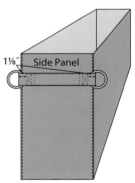

BIND THE ZIPPER ENDS

Prepare the Zipper Binding

1. Cut a strip of the main fabric 2″ × 22″. It can be on straight grain or on the bias; it doesn't matter. Cut the last 1½″ of one end to a point, and run the strip through a 1″ bias tape maker to turn in the edges. (If you don't have a bias tape maker, follow the instructions for a four-fold strap on page 45.) This is the zipper binding.

2. Cut the strip into 4 lengths 5″.

3. Clip the corners of each seam allowance, from the end of each crease to 1″ down the raw edge of the fabric.

Attach the Zipper Binding

1. At each end of each side of the zipper, lay a binding piece right side up on the wrong side of the zipper tape, aligning the folded edge of the tape an even ⅛″ from the edge of the zipper chain (teeth). Use fabric gluestick, fusible tape, or basting spray to stick or fuse the tape into place, taking care to keep it straight until the last 1″ of binding toward the center of the zipper. Curve the last 1″ so that the end of the binding is off the edge of the zipper tape.

NOTE:

You could choose to sew the binding to the zipper in the traditional 2-step way (stitch it on from the wrong side of the zipper, fold it to the right side, and stitch it into place), but the fastest, most accurate method is to stick it into place and sew both sides at once.

2. Fold the binding around to the right side of the zipper tape, and stick or fuse it into place.

3. Stitch the binding to the zipper tape, 1/16″ from the folded edges, through all layers of zipper tape, binding, and seam allowance.

MAKE THE ZIPPER TABS

1. Cut 2 rectangles of interfacing 2″ × 3½″, and fuse each to a scrap of fabric.

2. Follow the instructions in Make the Zipper Tab (page 63) for each end of the zipper.

NOTE:

You won't be able to stitch over the end of a chunky metal or plastic zipper chain, but stitch as close to it as you can, and then pivot to stitch the second row of top stitching.

ATTACH THE ZIPPER

1. On the top edge of the side panels, use a fabric marker or a small nick to mark 1″ in from each side seam.

2. Measure and mark the halfway point on the back of the zipper tape. These marks will correspond with the center points of the bag front and back.

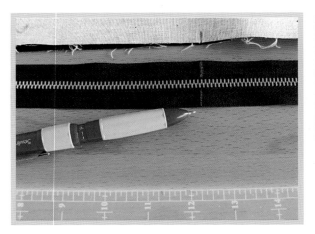

3. Take one side of the zipper tape and, with the right side of the zipper to the right side of fabric, match the center mark on the zipper tape with a CF/CB notch on the top edge of the bag. Pin the zipper and bag together at this point.

4. Align the zipper tape with the top edge of the bag, until you reach the marks on the side panels (1″ from the seam). At this point, twist the zipper ends in toward the inside of the bag. Pin or fuse the zipper tape and binding to the top of the bag to hold the zipper in this position.

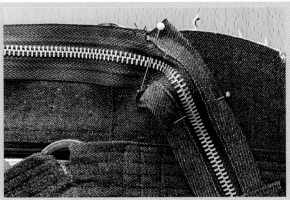

5. Stitch the zipper to the top edge of the bag, ¼″ in from the edge, stitching over the twisted end of the zipper tape so that the stitches do not catch the bound ends of the zipper tape to the bag.

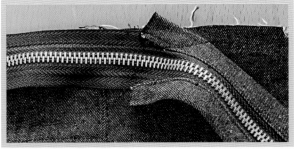

6. Repeat to attach the other side of the zipper tape to the other side of the bag.

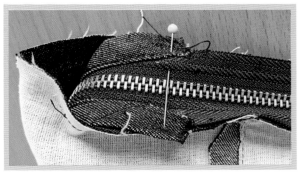

ATTACH THE FACING

1. Use the facing piece (cut from the piece that was slashed and opened), and follow the instructions to construct, attach, and understitch the facing (page 71). The zipper will be sandwiched between the facing and the bag, and the ends of the zipper will twist out of the seam (and hang freely) at each end.

2. Press the facing to the inside of the bag, pulling the fabric as far back from the zipper teeth as possible.

3. Topstitch around the top edge of the bag, ¼" to ⅜" from the top edge.

MAKE THE LINING

1. Follow the instructions (page 30) in Basic Bagmaking Techniques to add the compartment pocket to one of the lining pieces.

2. Follow the instructions in Exposed Zipper Pocket (page 36) to add an exposed zipper to the other lining piece.

3. Follow instructions in Basic Bag (page 74) to construct the lining, leaving a gap of at least 10" in the base seam.

ATTACH THE LINING

Follow the instructions (page 75) to attach the lining.

FINISH THE BAG

1. Follow the instructions (page 76) to anchor the lining base seams to the bag base seams.

2. Slipstitch (ladder stitch) to close the gap in the base seam of the lining.

3. Follow the instructions (page 46) to attach the shoulder straps to the rings on the side panel straps.

4. Give the bag a good press.

5. Feel really pleased with yourself as you look at your new bag.

THE SEOUL HANDBAG

FINISHED BAG: 12½" × 8½" × 4"

This cute everyday handbag is compact and functional, with internal and external pockets and a secure zippered closure at the top of the bag.

This project involves altering the pattern substantially to change the proportions and includes gusseted patch pockets on the front. Otherwise, it uses very basic techniques to construct the bag and its details. It comes together surprisingly quickly and is enormously satisfying to make.

PATTERN PIECES

- Front/Back bag body (pattern piece #1)
- Side panel (pattern piece #2)
- Facing (pattern piece #5)
- Lining (pattern piece #3)
- Lining side panel (pattern piece #4)
- Zipper pocket 3 facing (pattern piece #10)
- Bag base (pattern piece #6)
- Bag base support (pattern piece #7)
- Seoul pocket (pattern piece #14)
- Seoul pocket flap (pattern piece #15)
- Seoul pocket template (pattern piece #16)
- Seoul pocket flap template (pattern piece #17)
- Patch pocket (pattern piece #22)
- Straps and other components will be cut according to instructions.

MATERIALS

- 1 yard plain decor-weight or light denim fabric* (Don't use fabric that frays easily, or the external pocket will be too difficult to make.)
- ½ yard quilting-weight feature fabric
- ⅔ yard quilting-weight fabric for lining
- 1½ yards medium-weight woven fusible interfacing
- ⅔ yard medium-weight fusible fleece
- 6" × 13" Peltex, Timtex, or fast2fuse for bag base support
- 6" × 12" nonwoven fusible interfacing (Vilene S320 or Pellon Craft-Fuse) for zipper pocket lining
- 2 O-rings 1½"
- 1 metal slide adjuster 1½"
- 1 zipper 16" to match the main fabric
- 1 zipper 6" to match the 16" zipper, for the back of the bag

(continued on page 116)

Materials, continued

- 1 zipper 6" to match the lining (*optional*)

- ¼" fusible tape

- 2" × 12" fusible webbing

- Fabric gluestick

- Hera or disappearing marker

- Threads to match all fabrics

* I used fabric by Dear Stella.

ALTER THE PATTERN

1. Slash and close 5½" on horizontal slash line #1 on each of the following pattern pieces: bag body, lining, side panel, and lining side panel. (See Slash and Close, page 27.)

2. Slash and close 1¾" on horizontal slash line #2 on each of the following pattern pieces: bag body, lining, bag base, and bag base support.

3. Slash and close 1¾" on each vertical slash line #2 on the following pattern pieces: side panel, lining side panel, and facing.

4. Label the new pattern pieces carefully so that you won't mix them up with the other bag patterns.

5. Use the lining pocket pattern pieces from the basic bag pattern.

> ### NOTE:
> *You can choose to include any, all, or none of the lining pockets in this design, but you will need to shorten them to finish no deeper than 5½", so that they will fit inside the lining.*

FUSE AND CUT THE FABRIC

Prepare the Bag Body Pieces

1. Block fuse interfacing and fleece and cut 2 bag body pieces from the main fabric. Snip all the notches, and mark all of the dots on the wrong side of fabric (on the fleece).

2. Cut 2 facing pieces in the main fabric. You can either block fuse or cut the interfacing without seam allowances and then fuse.

3. Cut 1 bag base from the main fabric and cut 1 bag base support from fast2fuse, Timtex, or Peltex.

4. Block fuse the interfacing and fleece and cut 2 side panels in the feature fabric.

5. Cut lining, lining side panel, patch pocket, and zipper pocket 3 facing in lining fabric.

6. For the exposed zipper pocket on the back of the bag, cut 1 zipper pocket 3 facing in the main fabric.

7. Cut 2 zipper pocket 3 facings in nonwoven interfacing but do not fuse it to the fabric yet.

8. Cut a pocket in lining fabric, 8¼″ wide × 10″ deep, for an exposed zipper pocket on the lining of the bag.

9. Cut a pocket in lining or feature fabric, 8¼″ wide × 10″ deep, for the external pocket.

Prepare the Strap Pieces

1. Cut 2 O-ring loops 4″ × 4″ from the main fabric. Cut 2 interfacing strips 2″ × 4″. Center and fuse each strip of interfacing on the wrong side of an O-ring loop piece, with the length of the interfacing strip running along the straight grain of fabric.

2. Cut 1 shoulder strap 4″ × 40″ from the main fabric. Cut 1 interfacing strip 2″ × 37″ and fuse it, centered lengthwise and crosswise, on the wrong side of the strap piece.

Prepare the External Pocket Pieces

1. Cut 4 Seoul pocket pieces in feature fabric. Cut 4 Seoul pocket template pieces from interfacing, and fuse one centered on the back of each pocket piece. On the interfacing, mark 2 pieces "outer" and 2 pieces "lining."

2. Mark the notches on the curved bottom edge of each pocket with a scant ⅛″ nick, and mark the snap placement on the right side of each of the outer pieces.

3. Cut 2 Seoul pocket flap pieces in the main fabric and 2 in the feature fabric. Cut 4 Seoul

pocket flap template pieces from interfacing fabric, and fuse 1 to the back of each pocket flap piece.

4. For the pocket gussets, cut 2 strips of interfacing 1″ × 13″, and fuse them to the wrong side of the feature fabric, with the straight grain of fabric running along the length and with enough space to cut a ¼″ seam allowance around each strip.

5. Place the fabric (with the fused interfacing strips uppermost) on top of another layer of feature fabric, aligning the 2 fabrics on the same grain. Use a ruler and rotary cutter to measure and cut a ¼″ seam allowance around each of the interfacing pieces, through both layers of fabric. From here on, we'll call the interfaced pieces "outer" and the others "lining."

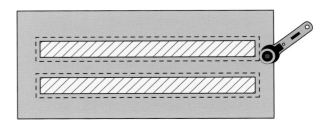

6. On the interfacing side of the outer gusset pieces, measure 4⁵⁄₁₆″ in from each short end, and draw a line across the width of the interfacing. Notch the seam allowances on either side of each line, with a scant ⅛″ nick.

7. Follow the instructions in Exposed Zipper Pocket (page 36) to mark and cut away the center of the interfacing for zipper pocket 3 facing, and then fuse it to the pocket facing.

THE EXPOSED ZIPPER POCKET

1. On the right side of the back bag body pieces, measure and draw a Hera or disappearing marker line 3″ from the top edge, across the middle 6″ of the piece.

2. Place the prepared pocket facing right side down on the right side of fabric, with the top edge of the facing aligned with the marker line.

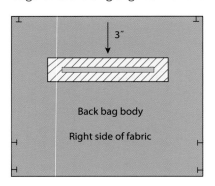

3″

Back bag body

Right side of fabric

3. Follow the instructions (page 36) for making the exposed zipper pocket. Remember to remove as much of the fleece as you can from the seam allowances of the zipper vent before pressing the facing to the inside of the bag piece.

NOTE:

Where the pocket instructions refer to "lining," read "outer bag fabric."

THE FRONT POCKETS

Make the Front Pockets

1. Match a top (squared) corner of each pocket piece with a short end of a pocket gusset (right sides of fabric together).

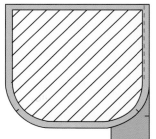

2. With the pocket piece uppermost on the sewing machine, stitch the pocket to the gusset, following the edge of the interfacing as a guide to the ¼″ seam allowance. As you near each curved corner, match the nick on the pocket to the corresponding nick on the gusset. Allow the outer edge of the seam allowance to flute slightly as you stitch around the edge of the interfacing.

3. Turn the pocket and gusset to the right side of fabric, with all the seam allowances folded toward the gusset. Edgestitch the gusset ⅟₁₆″ from the seam (catching the seam allowances to the underside).

4. Repeat Steps 1–3 to attach the pocket linings to the gusset linings; then trim the seam allowances of all 4 pocket and lining pieces with pinking shears.

5. Match each pocket lining to a pocket outer, with right sides of fabric together. Align the seams and smooth the 2 pieces together with the linings on the inside of the outer pockets. Press the pockets in this position, allowing any excess fabric on the lining pieces to overhang the edge of the outer pocket pieces. Pin the pocket pieces together, and trim off the overhanging lining fabric.

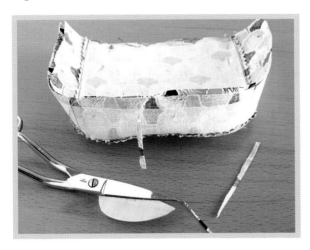

6. Stitch across the top and around the edge of the gusset, with a ¼″ seam allowance, to attach each outer pocket to its lining. Leave a 2½″ gap in the seam at the bottom of the gusset, to allow the pocket to be turned right side out.

7. On both pockets, use a small stitch to sew diagonally across each of the top corner seam allowances, crossing just inside (on the pocket side of) the corner point of the original stitch line. Trim off the seam allowance above this stitch line. This will help to make the corners turn through easily.

8. Turn the pockets through to the right side, and press them into shape. Use fabric gluestick, fusible tape, or fusible webbing to hold the gap in the bottom seam closed.

9. Topstitch all the way across the top edge of each pocket, ¹⁄₁₆″ from the top edge. Topstitch a second (parallel) row, ¼″ in from the first.

10. Attach the bottom half of a press snap to the marked point on each of the pockets.

Make the Pocket Flaps

1. Trim 1/16″ off the curved edges of each of the pocket flap linings.

2. Match each outer pocket flap piece to a flap lining piece, right sides together (with the lining side uppermost). Align the top edges of the outer fabric and lining, and stitch across the top with a 1/4″ seam allowance, leaving a 1 3/4″ gap in the middle of the seam for turning.

3. Pivot and sew around the curved edge of each flap, gently stretching the slightly smaller lining to the outer fabric without distorting the shape of the curve. The feed dogs of the machine will help to ease the outer fabric to the lining.

4. Stitch diagonally across the top corner seam allowances, crossing the corner just inside the existing stitch line, and then clip off the seam allowance above these stitches.

5. Use pinking shears to trim the seam allowances around the curved edge.

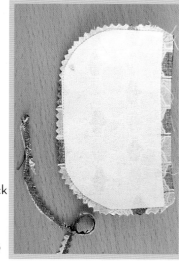

6. Turn both pocket flaps to the right side and press them flat. Use fabric gluestick or fusible tape or webbing to close the gap on the top edge of each.

7. Topstitch around the curved edge of each flap (from the right side of the outer flap) a generous 1/4″ from the edge.

8. Attach the top half of a snap closure on each pocket flap.

Attach the Patch Pockets

1. Across the right side of the bag body front, measure and draw a horizontal Hera or disappearing marker line 3/4″ above the base corner notch. Measure and draw a vertical line 1 1/4″ in from each of the side edges.

2. Place the pocket pattern so that the side edge lines up with a vertical marker line on the bag front and the bottom edge sits on the horizontal. Using a fine-point fabric marker or pencil, trace around the template to mark the pocket placement on the bag front. Mark the top corners of the pocket placement with a clearly defined dot or small horizontal line. Repeat for the other pocket placement.

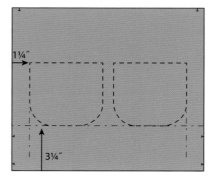

3. Use a rotary cutter and ruler to trim about 30″ of fusible webbing or tape to 1/8″ wide. It need not be all in one length.

4. On each pocket, carefully fuse the thin strips of webbing around the outer edge of the gusset, right near the seamed edge on the lining side.

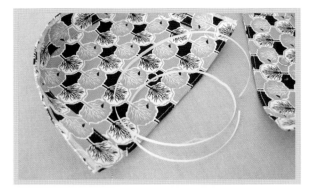

NOTE:

This can be a bit fiddly and the webbing will be quite fragile, but it gets easier with practice. I find it easier than pinning, but if you struggle too much with this step, try pinning or hand basting the pockets into place.

5. Remove the backing paper from the fusible tape, and align the edge of the gusset with the placement line. Carefully fuse and pin the pocket into position over the placement line (with pins at right angles to the edge of the gusset). The pins are necessary to reinforce the webbing.

6. Backstitching securely at each end, topstitch 1/16" from the edge of the gusset to attach each pocket to the bag front.

Attach the Pocket Flaps

1. Above each pocket on the front of the bag, place a pocket flap right side down, with the straight edge lying edge to edge with the top of the pocket. Pin both flaps in this position.

2. Stitch each pocket flap to the front of the bag, 1/16" from the straight edge. Pivot and stitch a second row, 1/4" above the first.

3. Give the pockets a press, snap the flaps closed, and admire your handiwork!

CONSTRUCT THE BAG BODY

1. With right sides of fabric together, match the front and back bag body pieces, and sew the base seam of the bag with a 1/2″ seam allowance.

2. Remove the fleece from the seam allowances, and then clip the corners to 1¼″ down the edge of the seam allowances. Press the seam open.

3. Follow the instructions to make and attach the external textile base (page 53).

4. Follow the instructions in The Basic Bag (page 66) to assemble the bag body. As you sew each side seam, remove all of the fleece and interfacing from the seam allowances, and press the seam allowances toward the center of the bag body. Edgestitch the bag body 1/16″ from the seam, catching the seam allowances to the underside.

THE STRAP

1. Follow the instructions (page 48) to make bagged-out O-ring loops.

2. Follow the instructions (page 46) to make a bagged-out shoulder strap with rings at both ends.

3. Then follow the instructions (page 50) to make an adjustable strap with the shoulder strap.

4. With the right side of the strap to the right side of the bag, center an O-ring loop over the center notch on the top edge of a side panel and pin it into place. Without twisting the strap, match the other O-ring loop to the same position on the other side panel. Stitch both O-ring loops into place, 1/4″ from the raw edge of the seam allowances.

THE ZIPPER GUSSET

1. Cut 2 interfacing strips 2″ × 12″, and follow the zipper gusset instructions (page 59) to make a narrow zipper closure for the top of the bag. (Each finished zipper gusset piece will be 1″ wide.)

2. Cut a rectangle of interfacing (or fast2fuse) 1½″ × 3″, and make a tab for the end of the zipper (page 63).

3. With the open end of the zipper to the left-hand side, place the zipper gusset right side down on the right side of the front of the bag. Align the raw edge of the zipper gusset with the top edge of the bag body. Center the gusset between the side seams, and pin it into place.

4. Open the zipper and match the other raw edge of the zipper gusset to the back of the bag body, right sides together and centered between the side seams. Pin the gusset into place, and then check that the zipper will close (make sure that there are no twists and that the strap is not caught on the wrong side of it).

5. Stitch the zipper gussets to the bag body pieces, ⅜" from the raw edge.

THE FACING

1. Follow the instructions in Basic Bag to construct and attach the facing (page 71).

2. Remove as much interfacing and fleece as you can from the seam allowance around the top of the bag and understitch, catching all of the seam allowances of the straps and zipper gusset to the underside of the facing.

3. Press the facing to the inside of the bag, topstitch around the bag ⅜" from the top edge, and then topstitch a row a scant ⅛" from the edge.

THE LINING

1. Follow the instructions to add an exposed zipper pocket (same dimensions as the external pocket, page 36) and a patch pocket (page 28) to the lining pieces. Place the patch pocket so that the top edge is ¾" from the top edge of the lining.

2. Follow instructions in Basic Bag (page 74) to construct the lining, leaving a gap of at least 7" in the base seam.

3. Follow the instructions (page 75) to attach the lining.

FINISH THE BAG

1. Follow the instructions (page 76) to anchor the lining base seams to the bag base seams.

2. Slipstitch (ladder stitch) to close the gap in the base seam of the lining.

THE GALAPAGOS BOHO

FINISHED BAG: 12¼" × 14" × 5"

This tall, soft, narrow shoulder bag exudes a strongly feminine style and is very practical. Its main feature is the large, darted pockets, and this project will show you a few tricks that will make these look super-professional and sharp. The zippered vent pockets will give your bag a tailored edge that will look anything but "homemade." The adjustable strap means that it can be carried high from one shoulder or draped across the body, hands free. The outer details take most of the sewing time with this project. The rest of the bag construction is quick and easy.

PATTERN PIECES

- Front/Back bag body (pattern piece #1)
- Side panel (pattern piece #2)
- Facing (pattern piece #5)
- Lining (pattern piece #3)
- Lining side panel (pattern piece #4)
- Bag base (pattern piece #6)
- Bag base support (pattern piece #7)
- Galapagos pocket (pattern piece #12)
- Galapagos pocket flap (pattern piece #13)
- Straps will be cut according to instructions.
- Choose any pocket pieces you want to include on the lining.

MATERIALS

- 1¼ yards quilting-weight fabric for outer bag*
- 1 yard quilting-weight fabric for lining
- ⅝ yard quilting-weight contrast fabric for pockets, straps, and pocket vents
- 1¾ yards medium- to heavy-weight fusible woven interfacing (Shape-Flex or heavier)
- ⅞ yard light fusible fleece
- 8" × 13" heavyweight fast2fuse for base support
- ⅔ yard lightweight woven interfacing
- 2 zippers 7" to match outer fabric

- 1 zipper 8" to match the lining fabric (*optional*, for lining pocket)
- 2 O-rings 1½"
- 1 slide adjuster 1½"
- 2 buttons 1" to coordinate with outer fabrics.
- ¼" fusible tape
- 3" × 12" fusible webbing (*optional*)
- Fabric gluestick
- Fine-point fabric pencil
- Disappearing marker pen or Hera marker
- Threads to match all fabrics

I used "Tonga" batiks by Timeless Treasures.

ALTER THE PATTERN

1. Slash and close 1″ on horizontal slash line #2 on each of the following pattern pieces: bag body, lining, bag base, and bag base support. (See Slash and Close, page 27.)

2. Slash and close 1″ on each vertical slash line #2 on the following pattern pieces: facing, side panel, and lining side panel.

3. Label the new pattern pieces carefully so that you won't mix them up with the other bag patterns.

4. You will need the Galapagos pocket and Galapagos pocket flap pieces from the provided pattern. Also use the compartment pocket and one of the zipper pocket pieces of your choice for the lining of the bag, if you wish.

FUSE AND CUT THE FABRIC

Prepare the Bag Pieces

1. Block fuse medium-weight interfacing to the main fabric; then fuse light fusible fleece to the interfacing, and cut 2 each of the bag body and side panel. Block fuse the interfacing only (not the fleece) and cut 2 facing pieces.

2. Block fuse lightweight interfacing to the contrast fabric, and cut 2 each of the Galapagos pocket and Galapagos pocket flap pieces.

3. Cut another set of 2 each of Galapagos pocket and Galapagos pocket flap in lining or contrast fabric, and then trim 1/16″–1/8″ from all the edges.

4. Cut the bag base in main or contrast fabric, and cut the bag base support in heavyweight fast2fuse. Center the fast2fuse on the wrong side of the bag base, and fuse it into place.

5. Cut 2 each of the lining and lining side panel, and then cut the pockets you'd like to make on the lining.

6. Cut 2 pocket linings 8½″ × 13″ from the lining or contrast fabric for the outside zippered pockets.

Prepare the Straps

1. For the side panel straps, cut 2 pieces 5″ × 18″ in the contrast fabric. Cut 2 medium-weight interfacing pieces 2½″ × 17″. Fuse the interfacing down the center of each strap (on the wrong side of fabric), leaving 1″ of fabric at one end without interfacing.

2. In the main fabric, cut 1 shoulder strap 4¼″ × 38″. Cut interfacing 2½″ × 36″ and fuse it, centered along the wrong side of the strap fabric.

THE SIDE PANEL STRAPS

Construct the Side Panel Straps

1. Using the 5″ × 18″ straps, follow the instructions to press in preparation to make a four-fold strap (page 45).

2. Open the strap folds again, and at the end of the strap that has no interfacing, cut away a 1″ square from each of the corners of the inner layers. We'll call this end the *reduced* end. Fold it again and press the strap as before.

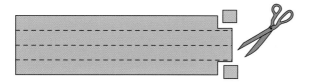

3. Measure 5″ from the reduced end, and mark a Hera or disappearing line across each strap.

4. Topstitch 1/16″ from each edge of each strap between the reduced ends and the marker line, backstitching neatly at each end of the stitch line.

5. Topstitch the full length of each strap, 3/8″ in from the outer top stitching (or a scant 1/2″ from the outer edge of the straps).

6. Thread the reduced end of each strap through an O-ring, and fold it 3″ from the end. Pin the end back onto the main strap, enclosing the ring in the loop.

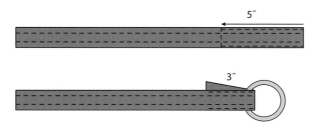

Attach the Side Panel Straps

1. Pin or fuse a strap (vertically) through the center of each side panel, aligning the raw end at the bottom of the strap (the end without the O-ring) with the bottom edge of the side panel.

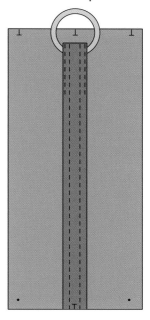

TIP:

For each side panel strap, cut a strip of fusible webbing 1¼″ × 11¾″. Fuse it from the bottom edge of the strap to the area underneath the folded end of the strap. Remove the backing paper, and fuse the folded end of the strap into place, pushing the outer edges of the folded end at least 1/16″ in from the sides of the strap. This will ensure that no raw edges will show when the straps are attached to the bag.

2. Measure and draw a Hera or disappearing marker line across each strap, 1¾″ below the folded edge of the O-ring loop. Measure and draw another line 1½″ below the first line on each strap.

3. On each strap, topstitch 1/16" from the edge, from the bottom of the strap to the top Hera marker line. Stitch an X-in-a-box between the 2 marker lines to anchor the straps firmly to the side panels, and then stitch down the other side of the strap 1/16" from the edge.

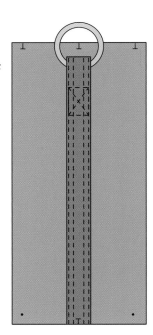

NOTE:

Stitch the X-in-a-box in a continuous line, stitching over an existing line of stitching as is necessary. This is neater and more durable than stopping and starting and backstitching.

THE DARTED PATCH POCKET

Construct the Pocket

1. Fold the fabric of each pocket and pocket lining piece, right sides together, to match the edges of each dart. Stitch the darts in a straight line 1/4" from the raw edge, backstitching neatly when you reach the fold of fabric above the dart. Clip the bottom corners of each dart seam allowance to 1/2" from the end of the seam.

2. On the outer fabric pieces, press the seam allowances of the darts toward the center of each pocket piece. On the lining pieces, press the seam allowances toward the outer edges.

3. Place each outer and lining pocket piece right sides together. The lining will be smaller than the outer, but match them together at the top corners and darts, and pin them at these points, with pins perpendicular (not parallel) to the edge of fabric.

4. With the lining piece on the top, align the outer edges of the pocket and lining (allowing the feed dogs to gently ease the outer to the lining, or slightly stretching the lining as necessary. Stitch with a 1/4" seam allowance around, except leave a 2 1/2" gap at the bottom edge of the pocket.

5. Stitch a diagonal line across each of the top corners of the pockets, beginning on the side seam allowances 3/4" from the top edge and finishing on the top edge, 1/2" from the corner point. Trim off the excess seam allowance above this stitch line.

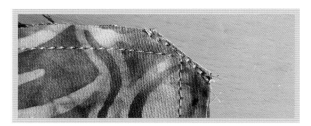

6. Trim the seam allowances (except where the opening in the seam is) with pinking shears.

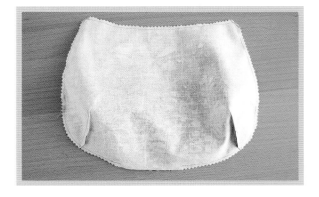

7. Turn the pocket through to the right side and press it. The lining should sit slightly inside the outer edge of the pocket.

8. Topstitch across the top of each pocket piece, ¹⁄₁₆″ from edge. Topstitch another row, a generous ¹⁄₄″ from the first row.

CONSTRUCT THE POCKET FLAP

Make the Button Loops

1. Cut a 6″ (straight-grain) strip of main fabric, ¹⁄₂″–³⁄₄″ wide, and fold it in preparation to make a small four-fold strap (page 45).

TIP:

Use a ¹⁄₄″ bias tape maker to fold tiny button loops from straight grain. Fuse ¹⁄₄″ fusible tape to the wrong side of the bias tape, and then fold and fuse it together.

2. Use a zigzag stitch the full width of the button loop (from edge to edge) to hold all the layers of the button loop strap together.

3. Cut the 6″ length into 2 pieces 3″, and fold each of these in half, matching the raw edges together.

4. Place each of the folded button loops on the right side of an outer pocket flap piece, matching the raw ends of the loop to the seam allowances at the center of the curved edge. Stitch the raw ends of the loops to the seam allowances of the flap, taking care not to stitch outside the ¹⁄₄″ seam allowances.

5. Match each outer pocket flap piece (right sides together) with its lining piece. Follow the same method as for the pocket to gently ease the lining to each of the outer pieces. Leave a 2¹⁄₂″ gap in the middle of the straight edge.

6. Stitch across the corner points at the top of each flap in a diagonal, from ³⁄₄″ on the side (curved) edge to ¹⁄₂″ along the top (straight) edge. Trim away the excess seam allowance above the diagonal stitch lines.

7. Trim the seam allowances of the curved edge (not the straight edge) with pinking shears, and turn the pocket flap through to the right side.

8. Press the pocket flaps flat and topstitch around the curved edge, ¹⁄₁₆″ from the edge. Topstitch another row a generous ¹⁄₄″ from the first row.

Attach the Pocket

1. Measure 3¾" from the bottom edge of the front and back bag body pieces, and draw a 3" Hera or disappearing marker line horizontally in the middle of the bag.

2. Use fabric gluestick or fusible tape to close the gap in the seam on each of the pocket and flap pieces.

3. Fuse ¼" fusible tape on the lining side, around the curved sides and bottom of each pocket piece.

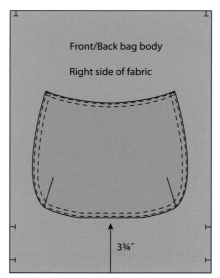

Front/Back bag body

Right side of fabric

3¾"

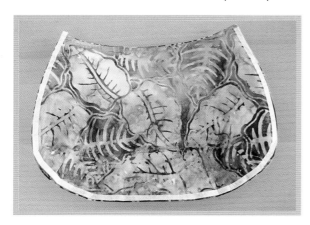

4. Remove the backing paper from the fusible tape, and place each of the pocket pieces on the right side of a bag body piece, aligning the bottom edge with the 3" line. Center the pocket horizontally (equal distance in from each side edge), and press to fuse it to the bag body.

5. Beginning in the top-right corner of the pocket, topstitch ¹⁄₁₆" from the edge around to the top-left corner. Pivot and stitch a U-turn; then stitch another row of top stitching a generous ¼" in from the first.

Attach the Pocket Flap

1. Fuse tape on the outer side of the flap, across the top straight edge. Remove the backing paper.

2. Place the pocket flap right side down on the right side of fabric, just above the pocket. Align the straight edge of the pocket just above (flush with) the top corners of the pocket. The flap will be upside down and lining side up. Press to fuse in place.

3. Topstitch 1/16" from the straight edge to attach the pocket flap to the bag body; pivot and stitch another row of top stitching a generous 1/4" in from the first.

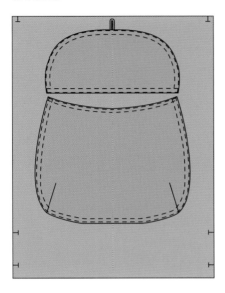

4. Fold the flap down over the top of the pocket and press it into place.

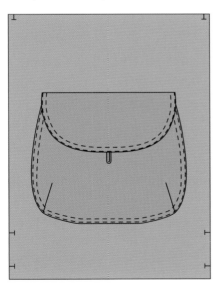

5. Mark a dot where the top of the button loop (where it attaches to the flap) sits on the front of the pocket.

6. Stitch a button in place, using an awl or matchstick to create some space between the button and fabric. Before tying off the thread, remove the matchstick or awl, and wrap the thread several times around the "shank" that is created in the space under the button.

TIP:

As you sew a button to the outside of the pocket, stitch through to a smaller (shirt) button on the inside. This will protect the fabric of the pocket from wear and tear when the bag is in use.

MAKE THE ZIPPERED WELT POCKET

This is an advanced method, and you may choose to completely ignore this feature, or else substitute with an exposed zipper pocket (page 36). You may prefer to practice this method on your lining (as an alternative to the exposed zipper pocket) before attempting it on the outside of the bag.

Make the Welts

1. Cut 4 strips of contrast fabric on the straight grain 1½″ × 8½″.

2. Fold each strip in half lengthwise, with right side of fabric facing out, and press a sharp crease. Slightly stretch the folded strip as you press. These are the welts for the pockets.

3. Machine stitch a scant ⅜″ from the long raw edge of each welt. Alternatively, fuse a strip of fusible webbing or tape into each piece, and press to hold the 2 raw edges together; then draw a fine fabric pencil line a scant ⅜″ from each raw edge. These are your stitch guidelines.

Attach the Welts

1. On the right side of each bag body piece, measure and draw a Hera or disappearing marker line 3″ below (and parallel to) the top edge. These lines mark the welt pocket placement.

2. Measure 3″ in from each of the side edges of the bag body pieces, and draw a 3″ vertical line across each end of the horizontal. These lines mark the edges of the welt pocket.

3. Center 2 welts on each bag piece, with the raw edges of the welts facing each other along the horizontal placement line. Pin them into place.

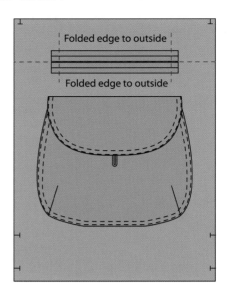

TIP:

Rather than pinning, I fuse a strip of ¼″ fusible tape over the placement line (finishing at the vertical lines) and fuse the welts into place.

4. Matching a ruler to the vertical lines on the bag body, draw in the end marker points on the welts with a fine-point fabric pencil.

5. With a small stitch, stitch along the horizontal stitch guidelines on each welt, starting and stopping exactly on the point where the vertical line crosses the welts. Backstitch neatly at each end.

6. Turn each bag piece to the wrong side, and check that the stitch lines are straight, exactly parallel, and finishing exactly at the end points. Fix any inaccuracies before proceeding.

7. On both bag body pieces, work from the wrong side of fabric to cut the fabric through the center of the space between the 2 stitch lines, stopping ¾" from the ends of the stitch lines.

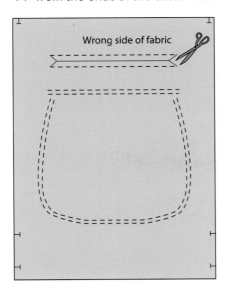

8. Taking care to cut *only the fabric of the bag* (not the welts), use your sharpest, snippiest scissors to snip at an angle to the ends of each stitch line. Then remove as much interfacing and fleece as you can from the seam allowances on both sides of the cut.

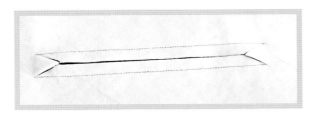

9. Pull the welts through to the wrong side of fabric, and turn the 2 folded edges to meet in the middle of the opening. Press the welts as you arrange them, and make sure that the corner points sit square.

10. Handstitch (tailor baste) the 2 folded edges of the welts together and press them.

11. Working from the right side of the bag body, fold each of the side edges (in turn) to expose the top of the welts and the little triangular shape at the end of each opening. Stitch across the wide base of each triangle to anchor the end point to the welts. (This can be done after the zipper is attached (below), but I prefer to secure the ends beforehand.)

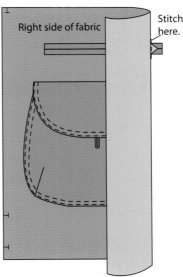

Attach the Zipper

1. Working on the wrong side of each bag piece, fuse ¼" fusible tape along the stitch line of each welt (centered over the stitches).

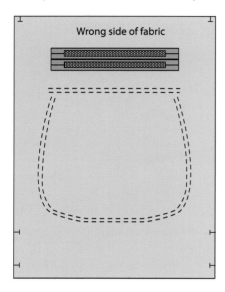

2. Remove the backing paper from the tape, and position a zipper with the chain/teeth running along the opening between the welts.

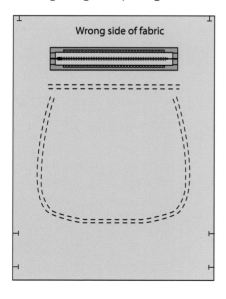

3. Cover the zipper and fabric with a piece of fabric or paper towel (to protect the iron from any exposed webbing while allowing steam to penetrate), and gently press with steam to fuse the zipper in place.

4. Turn the bag pieces to the right side and, beginning 2" from the end where the zipper head is sitting, stitch in-the-ditch of the seam that joins the top welt to the bag piece. Stitch around the end of the zipper and back toward the zipper head. As you near the zipper head, undo about a third of the basting stitches of the welt and move the zipper head out of the way, so that you can continue to stitch around that end of the welt and back to where you started.

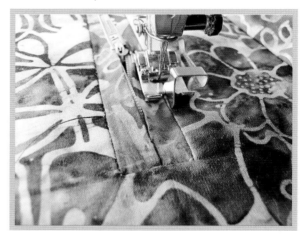

Attach the Pockets

1. Working on the wrong side of each of the bag pieces, place a pocket lining piece (right side down) over the welts. Align one of the short edges of the pocket lining to the raw edges of the lower welt seam allowances (with the pocket extending over the top edge of the bag), and pin or glue each pocket lining into place.

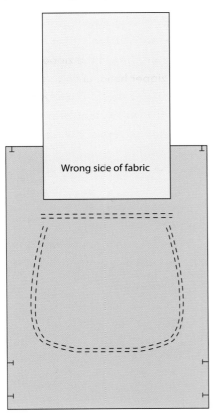

2. Holding the glued or pinned pocket and facing seam allowances, lift the bag piece up. Turn it over so that the pocket lining is under the bag body piece, and then fold the bag body back to expose the stitch line that attaches the lower welt.

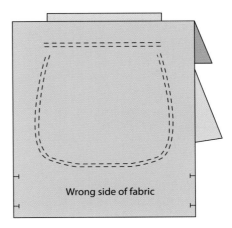

Use this stitch line as a guide to stitch the pocket lining to the welt. A narrow zipper foot will help you to get as close as you need to the stitch line.

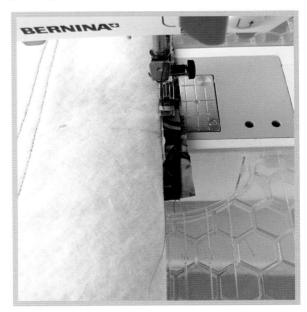

3. Fold the pocket down (to expose the back of the zipper) and press the seam flat. Match the other end of the pocket lining to the seam allowance of the upper welt. Pin or glue the pocket lining and welt seam allowances together, and then press the pocket to crease the fold line.

4. Use the same method as in Step 3 to attach the pocket lining to the upper welt.

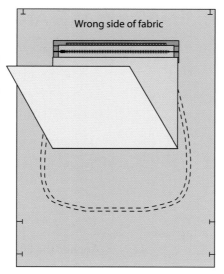

MAKE THE BAG BASE

Follow the directions (page 53) for the external textile base.

CONSTRUCT THE BAG BODY

Follow the instructions in Basic Bag (page 66) to continue constructing the bag body. As you sew each side seam, remove fleece and interfacing from the side seams, clip the seam allowances using the corner rule (page 21), and press the side seam allowances toward the center of the bag body. Topstitch on the bag body side, 1/16" from the seam, catching all the seam allowances to the underside of the fabric.

5. Working from the right side of the bag body pieces, fold each of the side edges in to expose the sides of the pocket lining. On both sides of each pocket, stitch across the triangle ends of the welt openings, through the zipper ends and pocket lining, and then stitch down to the folded edge at the bottom of the pocket lining.

MAKE AND ATTACH THE FACING

Follow the instructions in Basic Bag (page 71) to make and attach the facing to the top edge of the bag.

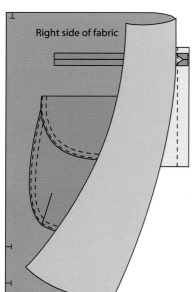

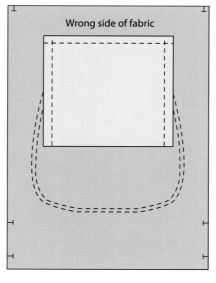

6. Take out the hand-basting stitches in the pocket vents and press them again.

INSERT THE MAGNETIC SNAP

Follow the instructions (page 58) to insert a magnetic snap in the facing.

MAKE THE LINING

1. Follow the instructions (pages 28–36) to add the pockets of your choice to the lining pieces.

2. Follow the instructions in Basic Bag (page 74) to construct the lining.

3. Follow the instructions (page 75) to attach the lining to the facing.

MAKE AND ATTACH THE SHOULDER STRAP

1. Follow the instructions (page 46) to make a bagged-out strap with a ring at both ends, using the long shoulder strap piece.

2. Then follow the instructions (page 50) to make an adjustable strap from your shoulder strap, attaching it to the O-rings on the side panels of the bag.

FINISH THE BAG

1. Anchor the lining to the base seams of the side panels (page 76).

2. Slipstitch (ladder stitch) to close the gap in the base seam of the lining.

3. Swan about and feel glamorous with your new bag!

THE BARCELONA SATCHEL

FINISHED BAG: 12½" × 11" × 6½"

This cute, little bag is made for working with the tailored glamour of bygone times. The handle detail combines leather-working and fabric-sewing techniques to produce a refined corded strap with O-rings and rounded tabs. The bag is made with stiff interfacing (fast2fuse) and a structured base. It requires a sturdy sewing machine, the ability to follow instructions closely, and the confidence to manipulate fabric that doesn't necessarily want to be manipulated.

Making the project is enormously satisfying. Although it's challenging, the finished bag looks sharp and professional—you won't be able to stop admiring your handiwork!

PATTERN PIECES

- Front/Back bag body (pattern piece #1)
- Side panel (pattern piece #2)
- Facing (pattern piece #5)
- Lining (pattern piece #3)
- Lining side panel (pattern piece #4)
- Bag base (pattern piece #6)
- Bag base support (pattern piece #7)
- O-ring tab (pattern piece #18)
- Straps will be cut according to instructions.
- Choose any pocket pieces you want to include on the lining.

MATERIALS

- ½ yard decor-weight feature fabric for outer bag*
- ⅞ yard contrast fabric (medium-weight denim or cotton drill)
- ⅛ yard plain, light fabric, color-matched to contrast fabric (for the backs of O-ring tabs)
- 1½ yards quilting-weight fabric for lining (You may need less, depending on the pockets you choose to use.)
- ⅛ yard Pellon Craft-Fuse, Vilene S320, or similar interfacing
- ⅞ yard heavyweight fast2fuse

- ¾ yard medium woven interfacing (Pellon Shape-Flex or similar)
- ⅞ yard light fusible woven interfacing
- 7" × 13" pelmet interfacing (Vilene S520 or Pellon Deco-Fuse) for bag base support
- 4 O-rings 1"
- 16" zipper to match contrast fabric
- 26" of ⅜"-diameter soft piping cord
- Sheet of template plastic
- Scraps of fusible fleece
- 7" × 23" fusible webbing
- ¼" fusible tape

(continued on page 140)

Materials, continued

- Fabric gluestick
- Scotch tape
- Pinking shears
- Fine-point fabric pencil
- Bulldog (binder) clips
- Disappearing marker pen or Hera marker

* I used "Fans" by Yardage Design.

NOTE:

Stiff interfacings, such as fast2fuse, give a smooth, structured shape to a bag. They also make the fabric more difficult to manipulate around the sewing machine. If you'd rather not face that challenge, you could block fuse Pellon Craft-Fuse or Vilene S320 and medium-weight fusible fleece to give the fabric more flexible support.

ALTER THE PATTERN

1. Slash and close 1" on horizontal slash line #2 on each of the following pattern pieces: bag body, lining, bag base, and bag base support. (See Slash and Close, page 27.)

2. Slash and close 1" on vertical slash line #2 on the following pattern pieces: facing, side panel, and lining side panel.

NOTE:

If you have made the Galapagos Boho (page 124), you can use the same patterns for any piece that requires 1" taken out of horizontal slash line #2 and vertical slash line #2. You may then simply make the horizontal slash line #1 adjustment.

3. Slash and close 4" on horizontal slash line #1 on the following pattern pieces: bag body, lining, side panel, and lining side panel.

4. Move the compartment pocket notch up 1" on the lining pattern.

5. If using the compartment pocket or divider pocket, slash and close 2" from horizontal slash line #1 (or simply shorten it from the bottom edge). Shorten the basic bag pocket by 2".

6. Label the new pattern pieces carefully so that you won't mix them up with the other bag patterns.

FUSE AND CUT THE FABRIC

1. Cut 2 bag body pieces from the feature fabric and from light fusible woven interfacing. Do not fuse them together.

2. Cut 2 fast2fuse pieces 12½" × 13", and center each piece on the adhesive side of an interfacing piece (with an even ½" seam allowance of interfacing visible around the fast2fuse). Place the bag body piece on top of the fast2fuse, and align its edges with the edges of the interfacing. Press from both sides of the fabric to align and fuse the interfacing and fast2fuse to the fabric.

3. Cut 2 strips 23" × 3¼" in contrast fabric, along the lengthwise grain of the fabric, for the straps.

4. Block fuse medium-weight interfacing to the contrast fabric, and cut 2 side panel pieces.

5. Cut 2 facing pieces in contrast fabric. Cut medium-weight interfacing without seam allowances (18½″ × 2″) and fuse it to the cut facings.

6. Cut the bag base in contrast fabric.

7. For the O-ring tabs, cut a piece of contrast fabric 12½″ × 6½″. Cut a strip of fast2fuse ½″ × 14″ and cut 4 circles of fusible fleece 1¾″ diameter. Place the 20″ plain lightweight fabric with this group of materials.

8. Cut the bag base support in pelmet interfacing (Vilene S520 or Pellon 520F Deco-Fuse) and template plastic.

9. Cut 2 each of the lining and lining side panel, and then cut any pockets that you'd like to include on the lining.

HANDLES

These corded strap handles are similar to the folded straps in the Marrakesh Overnighter (page 94), but they have the addition of ⅜″-diameter piping cord. This requires a sturdy sewing machine (preferably with the ability to move needle positions), and it takes a little more dexterity to manipulate the fabric.

If you'd rather simplify the handles, you can omit the cord and make a simple folded strap handle. Alternatively, you could make (even simpler) four-fold straps (page 45) for this bag.

Prepare the Outer Handle

1. Cut 2 interfacing pieces (preferably Vilene S320 or Pellon Craft-Fuse) 18″ × 1½″.

2. Cut a strip of light fabric 20″ × 2″ (with straight grain running along the length) for the inner straps.

3. Cut 2 pieces of paper-backed fusible webbing 23″ × 1½″. Use a rotary cutter and ruler for best (and speediest) results.

4. Draw a line 4″ in from each short end of the webbing. On each short end, measure and mark ¼″ in from the sides. Draw a diagonal line between the 4″ line on the long edges and the ¼″ mark on the short ends. Cut along the diagonal lines to taper the ends of the webbing as shown.

4″   Fusible webbing 23″ × 1½″   4″   ¼″ ¼″

TIP:

To save time cutting the ends of the fusible webbing, mark the end of one piece and then layer all the ends in careful alignment. Tape them to a cutting board, and use a rotary cutter to cut through all layers.

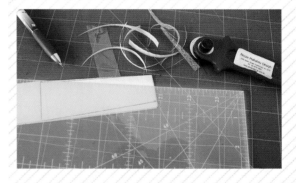

5. Center an interfacing strip on each of the 23″ × 3¼″ contrast strap pieces, on the wrong side of fabric. There should be 2½″ of strap showing on each short end and an even ¾″ seam allowance along each of the long edges. Fuse it into place.

6. Fuse the fusible webbing over the top of the interfacing, with the tapered ends of the webbing extending to the short ends of the strap. Leave the

backing paper on, and trim off the corners of inter-facing that peek out from behind the webbing.

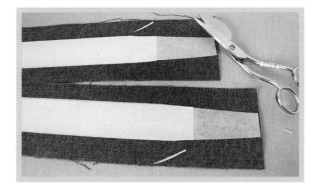

7. Using the backing paper of the fusible webbing as a fold line, turn and press the seam allowances over the top of the webbing and interfacing. Press the strap very flat to make the creases as sharp as possible. Snip $3/8$″ into the seam allowances at the 4″ mark from each strap end. This will help the seam allowances to sit flat around the tapered end of the strap.

8. On the tapered ends of each strap, trim the seam allowances from the end of the crease to about 2″ in from each short end. Then trim the rest of the seam allowance to an even $3/4$″.

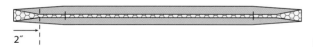

2″

9. Peel the backing paper off the straps and, placing them webbing-side down on an appliqué mat or baking paper, press them to stick all of the seam allowances into place.

Prepare the Inner Straps

1. Fold and press the inner strap piece as if to make a four-fold strap, but then open the center fold and press the strap flat, with the raw edges of fabric at the center on the underside.

TIP:

Use a 1″ bias tape maker to quickly turn the raw edges of the inner strap to the center.

2. Cut the strap into 4 pieces 5″ each, and then clip each of the corner seam allowances from the end of the creases to 1″ down the long, raw edges.

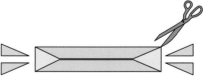

3. Spray the straps with quilt-basting spray (or cut strips of fusible webbing a scant 1″ × 5″, and fuse one to the back of each inner strap), completely covering the raw edges of fabric.

4. Working on the wrong side of the straps, stick/fuse an inner strap over the last 5″ of raw edges at each end.

Construct the Strap

1. Using a Hera or disappearing fabric marker, draw a line across the strap on the right side of fabric, 4½″ from each short end. Draw another line at the 4¼″ mark.

2. From the raw edge end of each strap, topstitch ¹⁄₁₆″ from the folded edge to the 4½″ line. Make a U-turn and topstitch a parallel line, a generous ¼″ from the first row of stitches, back to the raw edge. The stitches should catch the inner strap to the back of the strap.

3. Push each tapered strap end through an O-ring, and fold the end (inner sides together) to align the end of the strap with the other end of the inner strap, with the O-ring sitting in the fold. Pin, glue, or fuse the end of the strap into place.

4. At both ends of each strap, topstitch (from the right side of the strap) along the 4½″ line, back-stitching at each end of the stitch line. Pull all the excess threads through to the wrong side of fabric.

5. Cut another 2 strips of fusible webbing 1½″ × 15″, and center each over the inner side of a strap. Fuse the webbing and remove the backing paper.

6. Cut 2 pieces of ³⁄₈″-diameter piping cord 13″ each. Press the cord with a steam iron, and then stretch it to straighten it. Position each length over the fusible webbing, along the center of a strap.

7. Using a hot steam iron (and with bulldog clips at the ready), fold the strap over the top of the cord. While the fusible webbing is still warm, use your fingers to align and press together the folded edges of the strap. Use the bulldog clips to hold the edges together as you work. Allow the straps to cool.

8. It may take a bit of experimentation with your sewing machine, presser feet, and needle positions to find the best setup for this step, and you may need a larger needle (or denim needle). My machine works best with a ¼″ foot and the needle as far left as the foot will allow.

Work on both straps in turn. Beginning near the folded edge of the handle, hold the threads and backstitch neatly; then stitch across the 4¼″ line at one end, through all thicknesses of fabric. Pivot and then stitch the folded edges together, ¹⁄₁₆″ (or as close to it as you can) along the length of each strap. Pivot and stitch across the 4¼″ line at the other end of the strap. Backstitch to secure the ends of the stitching.

9. Change to a narrow zipper foot, and stitch as close to the cord as you can, the full length of the cord, backstitching neatly at both ends.

Construct the O-Ring Tabs

1. Use pattern piece #18 to cut 4 O-ring tab pieces in nonwoven interfacing (preferably Vilene S320 or Pellon Craft-Fuse).

2. Fuse the interfacing pieces to the plain, light fabric, with enough space around each for a ¼" seam allowance.

3. Place the contrast fabric and the plain light-weight fabric right sides together, and press them together to eliminate all wrinkles and puckers.

4. Using the outer edge of each piece of interfacing as a guide, carefully stitch around the sides and curved bottom of each tab shape. Leave the top, straight edge of each tab open.

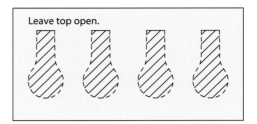

5. Cut each tab out, using pinking shears. The inner points of the shears should be approximately ¹⁄₁₆" from the stitches.

6. Pinch the interfacing side of each tab to separate it from the contrast fabric layer, and snip a 1" vertical slit into the center of the circular area. Snip a 1" horizontal slit across the vertical one, and use this hole to turn each tab through to the right side. Turn the edges of each tab through as smoothly as possible, and press each one flat.

7. Push a circle of fusible fleece through the snipped hole in the back of each O-ring tab, with the fusible side toward the back of the contrast fabric. Make it sit flat and then press the tab to fuse it into position.

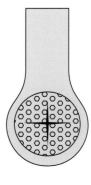

8. Cut the ½″ strip of fast2fuse into 4 equal lengths, and thread each one through the top opening in an O-ring tab, so that it sits in the "neck" of the tab and extends between the fleece and the slits in the light fabric layer. Press to fuse all the layers together.

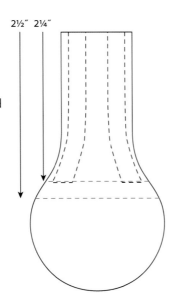

9. On the right side of each tab, measure and draw a Hera or disappearing marker line 2½″ from the top of the neck. Draw another line ¼″ above each of these lines (at the 2¼″ mark).

10. Topstitch 1/16″ from the edge, from the end of the neck to the 2¼″ marker line. Pivot, U-turn, and topstitch back to the top edge, ¼″ in from the first.

Attach the Straps

1. Fold and press each O-ring tab 1½″ from the end of the "neck." Making sure that the right side of the tab is facing the same direction as the corded side of the strap, thread an O-ring over the folded end of each tab, and pin the end in place on the back of the tab.

2. From the right side of the tab, topstitch across the 2½″ marker line. Backstitch neatly and pull the threads to the back.

3. Measure and mark a Hera or disappearing marker line 3¼″ from the top edge, across the right side of both bag body pieces. Between this line and the top of the bag, draw lines 3″ from each of the side edges. These are placement lines for the tabs.

4. Position each of the 4 tabs with the bottom edge at the horizontal line and the (outer) side edge at the vertical line. Pin, glue, or fuse the tabs into place.

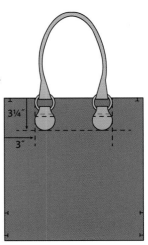

TIP:

Hold the O-ring tabs, and curve the straps in both directions. You may notice that the curve is smoother in one particular direction. Place the handle on the bag with the strap sitting in the smoothest possible curve.

5. Topstitch ¹⁄₁₆″ in from the edge of each tab, and across the 2¼″ marker line, to attach them to the bag pieces. Pivot or reverse (so that you don't have to stop and start) and stitch a second row ¼″ in from the first. Pull all the threads to the wrong side of fabric.

MAKE THE BAG BASE

1. On the pelmet interfacing, mark the purse feet positions 1″ from the long edges of the base, 1¼″ in from each of the short ends, and in the center of the long horizontal placement lines.

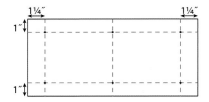

2. Follow the directions in Structured External Base with Purse Feet (page 55).

CONSTRUCT THE BAG BODY

1. Follow the instructions for the Basic Bag (page 66). Hold the bag pieces together as you sew with pins or bulldog clips. Stitch along the outer edge of the fast2fuse with a zipper foot—as close as you can without catching it in the seam. As you sew each side seam, remove the interfacing from the side panel seam allowances only (not the interfacing that is holding the fast2fuse in place).

2. Clip the seam allowances using the corner rule (page 21), and press the seam allowances open.

MAKE THE ZIPPERED CLOSURE

1. Cut 2 interfacing strips 2″ × 12″ and follow the zippered gusset instructions (page 59) to make the zipper closure for the top of the bag, using the contrast fabric and lining fabric.

2. Make a 1½″ × 3″ tab for the end of the zipper (page 63) in contrast fabric, and attach it to the very end of the zipper (just covering the metal stopper).

3. Center one side of the zipper gusset along the top edge of one side of the bag body, right sides of fabric together. Align the raw edges of the zipper gusset and the bag, and pin the gusset securely to the bag body. Use a zipper foot to stitch the gusset into place, ³⁄₈″ from the edge.

4. Open the zipper and, taking care not to twist it, place the other side of the zipper (right sides together) centered along the top edge of the other side of the bag. Pin securely and stitch ³⁄₈″ from the edge to hold it in place.

MAKE AND ATTACH THE FACING

1. Follow the instructions on the Basic Bag (page 71) to make and attach the facing to the top edge of the bag. Stitch along the outer edge of the fast2fuse with a zipper foot—as close as you can without catching it in the seam.

2. Understitch the facing (page 72), catching all the seam allowances of the zipper gussets in the stitches.

3. Press the facing to the inside of the bag, and topstitch only on the side panel pieces, ³/8″ from the top edge of the bag.

MAKE THE LINING

1. Follow the instructions (page 28) to add the pockets of your choice to the lining pieces.

2. Follow the instructions in Basic Bag (page 74) to construct the lining, but only sew 1³/4″ at each end of the base seam, as you'll need a large gap to turn this stiff bag through to the right side.

ATTACH THE LINING

Follow the instructions (page 75) to attach the lining to the facing, and turn the bag right side out.

FINISH THE BAG

1. Anchor the lining to the base seams of the side panels (page 76).

2. Slipstitch (ladder stitch) to close the gap in the base seam of the lining.

3. Pinch the side seams of the facing to pleat the top edge of the side panels inward. Press and pin

through the facing and all layers of the bag outer to hold the pleat in position.

4. Topstitch the facing ¼″ from the folded edge through all layers of fabric, from the top of the bag to the facing-lining seam.

5. Swing your unique bag and show your style.

THE LAHTI FLIGHT BAG

FINISHED BAG: 15½″ × 11″ × 6″

This bag is designed to hold all you'd need for a flight or for any other occasion when you need to carry a change of clothes, notebook computer, book, or craft project. It zips securely across the top and can be carried with a shoulder strap or by grab-handles. It has four external compartment pockets for easy access to your book, boarding passes, or snacks.

The bag is structured with a combination of fleece and nonwoven interfacing, which has springy structure that is easier to manage around a sewing machine than it appears. The shoulder strap and grab-handles are all based on the basic four-fold strap method, with reinforcements and rings for extra strength, comfort, and style. Because of the inclusion of the zippered top panel, the construction of this bag differs from the other projects, and the lining is attached from the top of the bag (with no facing). It's an excellent way to extend basic skills, because the success of this bag requires accuracy in cutting and sewing.

PATTERN PIECES

- Front/Back bag body (pattern piece #1)

- Side panel (pattern piece #2)

- Bag base (pattern piece #6)

- Bag base support (pattern piece #7)

- Straps and other bag components will be cut according to instructions.

- Choose any pocket pieces you want to include on the lining.

MATERIALS

- 1 yard quilting or light decor-weight feature fabric for outer bag*

- ⅓ yard coordinating print decor fabric for external pockets

- 1¾ yards quilting-weight contrast fabric (You will need this length to cut the shoulder strap, but you will have a lot of fabric left over for another project.)

- 1½ yards quilting-weight fabric for lining

- 1¾ yards yard light, stiff interfacing (Pellon Craft-Fuse or Vilene S320) for the bag body and internal pocket facing (if using)

- 1 yard medium-weight fusible fleece (Pellon 987F or Vilene H640)

- 7″ × 16″ pelmet interfacing (Vilene S520 or Pellon 520F Deco-Fuse) for bag base

(continued on page 150)

Materials, continued

- 1¾ yards medium-weight woven fusible interfacing (Shape-Flex) for the external pockets and straps

- 1 sheet template plastic

- 6 purse feet ½"

- 16" or 18" zipper to match main or contrast fabric

- 2 O-rings 1"

- 1 slide adjuster 1"

- 8" zipper to match lining fabric (*optional* for lining pocket)

- 5" × 18" fusible webbing

- ¼" fusible tape

- Fabric gluestick

- Quilt-basting spray

- Scotch tape

- Fine-point fabric pencil

- Disappearing marker pen or Hera marker

- Threads to match all fabrics

I used fabric by Echino.

ALTER THE PATTERN

1. Slash and close 1" on horizontal slash line #2 on each of the following pattern pieces: bag body, bag base, and bag base support. (See Slash and Close, page 27.)

2. Slash and close 1" on each vertical slash line #2 on the side panel.

3. Slash and open 3" on vertical slash line #1 on each of the following pattern pieces: bag body, bag base, and bag base support. (See Slash and Open, page 26.)

4. Slash and close 3" on horizontal slash line #1 on the bag body and side panel pattern pieces.

5. For the zippered top panels, take the altered bag base pattern, and draw a line through the center, lengthwise. Trace half of the bag base pattern, and then add a ¼" seam allowance along the edge that was previously the centerline.

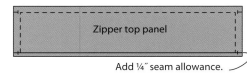

Add ¼" seam allowance.

6. If using the compartment pocket (pattern piece #8) or divider pocket (pattern piece #24), slash and open 3" on vertical slash line #1.

7. Label the new pattern pieces carefully—don't mix them up with the other bag patterns!

FUSE AND CUT THE FABRIC

Prepare the Bag Body

1. Block fuse light, stiff interfacing and then fleece to the feature fabric, and cut 2 bag body pieces and 2 side panel pieces. On the wrong side of fabric (on the fleece), mark the dots on the base corner, and snip all the notches.

> ### NOTE:
> *If all the pieces of the bag are to come together in a neat box shape, it's important to cut and mark them accurately. Even though the fleece will be removed from the seam allowances later, block fusing makes it easier to cut accurately, and in the long run, this will save you time.*

2. On the interfacing side of each bag body and side panel piece, mark a dot ½" in from the side and ½" down from the top edge (right on the corner of the 2 stitch lines). If it's easier, use the dot marking on the base corner of the side panel pattern as a template. (It measures the same distance from the corner point.)

3. Block fuse light, stiff interfacing (not fleece) to the feature fabric, and cut 2 zippered top panel pieces from the pattern created in Step 5 of Alter the Pattern (page 150).

4. Cut 2 zippered top panels in fusible fleece. Trim ¼" off one of the long edges on each piece. Leaving a ¼" seam allowance free of fleece on one long side, fuse a fleece piece to each of the outer fabric pieces of the top panel.

5. Cut the bag base in contrast fabric, and cut the bag base support in pelmet interfacing (Vilene S520 or Pellon 520F Deco-Fuse) and template plastic.

6. To make the front pockets, cut 2 rectangles in coordinating fabric and 2 in lining fabric, 8¾" × 16½". Cut 2 medium woven interfacing pieces 7¾" × 15½", and fuse them (centered) on the wrong side of the outer pocket pieces.

7. Use the outer bag body and side panel patterns to cut the lining and lining side panel, and then trim ¼" off the top edge of each. Mark the notches on the new top edge, using the pattern piece as a guide, and mark the stitch-line corner points (on each top corner) with dots on the wrong side of fabric.

8. Cut 2 zippered top panel pieces in lining.

9. Choose and cut the pockets you'd like to make on the lining (see Pockets, page 28).

Prepare the Straps

1. For the side panel straps, cut 2 straps 4¼" × 13" in the contrast fabric. Cut 2 fusible woven interfacing pieces 2⅛" × 12". Fuse the interfacing down the center of each strap (on the wrong side of fabric), leaving 1" of fabric at one end without interfacing.

2. Cut 2 handles 4¼" × 24" from the contrast fabric. Cut 2 woven fusible interfacing pieces 2⅛" × 22" and fuse them, centered, along the wrong side of each handle piece.

3. Cut 2 reinforcement straps 4¼" × 20" in contrast fabric. These need no interfacing.

4. Cut a shoulder strap 4¼" × 60" in contrast fabric. Cut woven fusible interfacing 2⅛" × 58" and fuse it, centered, on the wrong side of the strap.

SIDE PANEL STRAPS

Construct the Side Panel Straps

1. Using the 4¼" × 13" straps, follow the instructions to press in preparation to make a four-fold strap (page 45) with a ring at one end. At the end of the strap that has no interfacing, cut away the inner layers of the last ¾" to reduce bulk (page 20). Fold and press the strap again.

2. Measure 4" from the "reduced" end, and mark a Hera or disappearing line across each strap.

3. Topstitch ¹⁄₁₆" from each edge of each strap, between the raw ends and the 4" marker line, backstitching neatly at each end of the stitch line.

4. Topstitch the full length of each strap, ³⁄₈" from the outer edges of the straps.

5. Thread the reduced end of each strap through an O-ring, and fold it 2" from the end. Pin the end back onto the main strap, enclosing the ring in the loop.

6. Cut and fuse a 1" × 9" strip of fusible webbing to the wrong side of each strap, from the bottom raw end to just under the folded O-ring end.

Attach the Side Panel Straps

1. Working on the right sides of the side panels, fuse a strap (vertically) through the center of each side panel, aligning the raw edges of the strap and panel at the bottom edge and tucking the raw ends at the O-ring end out of sight (under the main strap).

2. Measure and draw a Hera or disappearing line across each strap, 1¼" below the folded edge of the O-ring loop. Measure and draw another line 1¼" below the first line on each strap.

3. On each strap, topstitch ¹⁄₁₆" from the edge, from the bottom of the strap to the top Hera line. Pivot and stitch an X-in-a-box between the 2 marker lines, and then stitch down the other side of the strap, ¹⁄₁₆" from the edge.

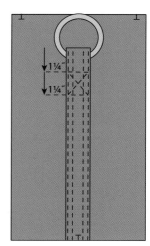

TIP:

To stitch a neat X-in-a-box, use a disappearing fabric marker and ruler to draw in the stitch line. Stitch in a continuous line to sew the X shape and across the marker lines that cross the strap. It doesn't matter if you stitch over an existing line of stitches. (It's still neater than backstitching.)

THE GRAB-HANDLES

Construct the Handle Straps

1. Follow the instructions (page 45) to make four-fold straps with the 4¼" × 24" straps. Topstitch the straps ¹⁄₁₆" from each edge, and then topstitch another row ¼" in from each of the outer rows. Trim off any rough edges and threads on the ends of the straps.

2. Follow the four-fold strap instructions to fold the 4¼" × 20" reinforcement straps, and topstitch each of them, ³⁄₈" in from each edge. (Do not stitch ¹⁄₁₆" from the edges.)

Attach the Handles

1. On the right side of each bag body piece, measure and mark a Hera or disappearing line 4″ below (and parallel to) the top edge. Measure 4½″ in from both ends of the horizontal line on each of the bag body pieces, and mark a 1″ vertical line toward the top edge of the bag.

2. On the right side of one of the bag body pieces, place a short, raw edge of a handle strap ⅛″ above the horizontal line, with the single-folded edge of the four-fold handle strap facing toward the center of the bag and the double-folded edge of the strap aligned with the short vertical line. Pin the strap end in this position.

3. Without twisting the handle strap, match the other raw end to the same position on the opposite side of the bag body. Pin it into place, and repeat this to place the other handle on the other bag body piece.

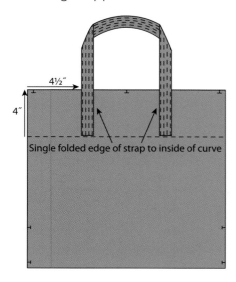

4. Stitch across the handles, ½″ from each of the raw ends, to hold them securely in position on the bag body pieces.

Reinforce the Grab-Handles

1. Trim the reinforcement straps to 16½″ long, and keep the leftovers to use as zipper-end tabs for the top of the bag.

2. Fuse 1″ strips of fusible webbing (or hemming tape) along the full length of each of the reinforcement straps. Place each reinforcement strap across the right side of a bag body piece, aligning the bottom edge of the strap with the horizontal marker line and covering the ends of the handles. Fuse the reinforcement straps into place.

TIP:
Take the time to check that both straps have the single-folded edge to the top. It looks neater this way.

3. Topstitch 1/16″ in from each edge of the reinforcement straps to attach them to the bag body pieces.

4. At the base of each handle, stitch an X-in-a-box.

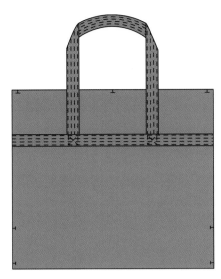

THE EXTERIOR POCKETS

Make the Pocket Pieces

1. Match each front pocket piece, right sides together, to a pocket lining piece, and stitch across the top edge with a 1/2″ seam allowance.

2. On both pockets, trim the seam allowances at each end using the corner rule (page 21).

3. Turn the fabric to the right side. Fold all the seam allowances toward the lining side of the seam (on the underside) and understitch the lining, 1/16″ from the seam.

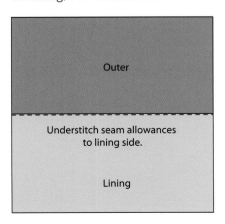

Outer

Understitch seam allowances
to lining side.

Lining

4. Fold the lining and outer pocket pieces along the seamline, with wrong sides together, and press them flat.

TIP:

Use quilt-basting spray to hold the pocket and pocket lining fabrics together.

5. Topstitch along the top edge of the pocket, 1/16″ from the edge, and then topstitch a second row, 1/4″ in from the first.

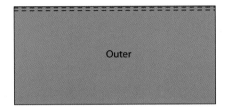

Outer

6. On the right side of the outer pocket fabric, measure and mark a Hera or disappearing marker line 8 1/8″ in from one of the side edges. Measure and draw another line 8 1/8″ in from the other side.

Attach the Pockets

1. On the lining side of each pocket piece, fuse 1/4″ fusible tape (or use fabric gluestick) along the side and bottom edges. Also fuse tape on the lining side, aligned between the 2 marker lines on the right side of fabric, in the center of the pocket.

2. Fuse (or glue) the pockets into place, right side up on the right side of each of the bag body pieces, matching the side edges and aligning the top edge of the pocket 1/16″ below the bottom edge of the reinforcement strap.

3. Use a walking foot, if you have one, to topstitch over the marker lines that divide each pocket into 2 pieces. Stitch from the bottom edge, pivot, and U-turn to stitch along the second line, back toward the bottom edge of the pocket.

4. Reinforce the pocket with a zigzag stitch across the bottom edge of fabric, securing it to the bag body and stopping the raw edge from fraying.

MAKE THE BAG BASE

1. On the pelmet interfacing, mark the purse feet positions 1¼″ from the long edges of the base, 1¼″ in from each of the short ends, and in the center of the long horizontal placement lines.

2. Follow the directions for the Structured External Base with Purse Feet (page 55).

CONSTRUCT THE BAG BODY

1. Follow the instructions for constructing the basic bag (page 66), with one minor change. Working on one seam at a time, pin through the dots at the top and bottom corners to hold each side panel to the bag body, and sew each side seam only between the pins. Backstitch neatly to secure every seam end. The seam allowance at the top edge of the bag must not be included in the seam.

NOTE:

The stiffness and springiness of the bag can make this stage quite awkward. Use as many pins or bulldog clips as you need to hold each seam into place before you sew (with the pins perpendicular to the fabric edge, not parallel).

2. Remove fleece (and as much interfacing as you can) from every side seam, but don't clip the corners of the seam allowances yet.

3. Press the side seam allowances open, and sew the base seam.

MAKE THE ZIPPERED TOP PANEL

1. Place the zipper facedown on the right side of an outer zipper top panel piece. Match the edge of the zipper tape with the raw edge of the ¼″ seam allowance (and the chain/teeth of the zipper on the fabric), and align the metal stopper at the opening end of the zipper, ¾″ from the end of the panel. If you have used a zipper that is longer than 16″, let the closed end of the zipper run off the other end of the panel.

2. Stitch the zipper to the top panel piece, ¼″ from the edge of the zipper tape, the full length of the top panel.

3. Place a lining piece over the top of the panel piece, right sides of fabric together and with the zipper sandwiched between. Align all the outer edges, and stitch the lining into place, following the existing line of stitching on the zipper tape.

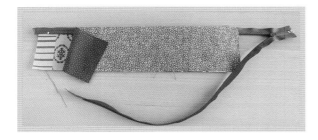

4. Fold the outer and lining fabrics away from the zipper, and press them wrong sides together, aligning all of the raw edges of fabric. Use quilt-basting spray to hold the lining and the outer fabrics together.

5. Topstitch the full length of the panel, 1/16" from the seam edge, and then topstitch another row 1/4" in from the first row.

6. Repeat Steps 1–5 to attach the zipper to the other side of the top panel and lining pieces.

7. Whipstitch the ends of the zipper tape together at the opening end of the zipper. If using a zipper longer than 16", zigzag a stopper level with the end of the panel pieces, and trim off the excess zipper.

8. Take the leftovers from the reinforcement straps, and topstitch 1/16" from each side edge. These are your zipper-end tabs.

9. Fold each zipper-end tab in half, matching the raw ends together. Match each tab to an end of the zipper, centering it and aligning the raw edges with the raw edges of the panel piece. Stitch the tabs into place 1/4" from the edge of the fabric.

10. Measure across the completed zippered top panel. It needs to measure 7", but is probably a little wider than that right now (depending on the width of the exposed area of zipper). With the zipper at the center of the panel, trim off the excess on both long edges so that its total width is 7" (so that it will match to the top edge of the side panels).

11. On the lining side of the zippered top panel pieces, mark corner points (1/2" in from each side) in the stitch line with disappearing marker dots.

ATTACH THE ZIPPERED TOP PANEL

1. With right sides together, match a long side of the zippered panel to the top edge on a side of the bag body. At each end of the top panel, align the stitch-line corner dots to those on the top panel, and pin them together. Use pins or bulldog clips to hold the panel in place before sewing.

2. Beginning on a dot, backstitch neatly and securely, and then stitch the top panel to the bag body with a ½″ seam allowance. Stop and back-stitch neatly on the dot on the next corner. Don't overshoot the dot—you need accuracy here.

3. Open the zipper and attach the other side of the top panel to the other side of the bag body. Again, take care to stitch with an even ½″ seam allowance, starting and stopping accurately on the dots.

4. With the zipper a third closed, align the short ends of the top panel with the top edge of the side panels. Match the stitch-line corner points, and pin them together. Backstitch securely, and sewing only between the corner-point dots, sew the top panel to the side panel pieces.

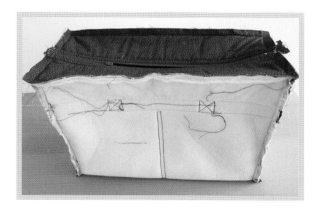

5. Remove what you can of the fleece and interfacing from the seam allowances of the top and side panels.

6. Without trimming the top panel at all, trim the corners of the side seam allowances (using the corner rule, page 21) to 1¼″ down the edge, at the top edge.

7. Trim the corners of the base and side seam allowances at the bottom corners.

MAKE THE LINING

1. Follow the instructions (pages 28–36) to add the pockets of your choice to the lining pieces.

2. Follow the instructions in Basic Bag (page 74) to construct the lining, but only stitch the side seams between the top-corner-point dots and the base-corner dots. Leave a large gap in the base seam (stitch only the last 1″–2″ of the base seam at each side) so that you'll be able to turn the bag through to the right side easily.

3. Clip the corners of the seam allowances at the bottom corners only, and press the side seam allowances open.

ATTACH THE LINING

1. With the bag and the lining both inside out, match the top edge of the lining to the lining side of the zippered top panel (right sides of fabric together). Match the long edges of the lining to the long edges of the top panel, and pin the top-corner dots on the lining to the corner dots on the top panel.

2. Beginning and ending (and backstitching securely) on the corner dots, sew the lining to the top panel with a ½″ seam allowance. It's easiest to work from the bag body side and follow the existing line of stitching.

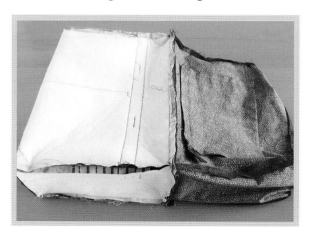

3. Repeat to sew the top edges of each side panel of the lining to the top panel.

4. Trim the corners of the seam allowance to reduce bulk, using the corner rule (page 21), and then press the seam allowances open (using a pressing ham, cloth, or whatever support you find most useful).

5. Turn the bag through to the right side of fabric, and anchor the lining to the base seams of the side panels (page 76).

6. Slipstitch (ladder stitch) to close the gap in the base seam of the lining.

THE SHOULDER STRAP

1. Using the 4¼″ × 60″ strap, follow the instructions to make a four-fold strap with rings at both ends (page 45).

2. Follow the instructions to make an adjustable strap (page 50), and attach it to the rings in the side panel straps.

3. Give your bag a final press, and get ready for an adventure!

THE MELBOURNE WEEKENDER

FINISHED BAG: 12½" × 10" × 5½"

This bag was inspired by public transport and busy city or university life. It's made in hard-wearing denim, with a long adjustable shoulder strap and a sturdy grab-handle, and it has the security of both zippered and twist-lock closures. The design is unisex, and the feature fabric can be changed to suit the personality of the wearer.

The grab-handle on this bag uses a turned-edge technique that is a leather-work method that has been adapted to woven fabric. This finely finished handle style allows you to create structure and strength using heavier fabrics (such as denim), without the difficulties caused by the buildup of fabric bulk. You'll have to concentrate on the instructions the first time you make the grab-handle, but with practice, you'll gain confidence, skill, and speed. If you want to simplify and speed up the sewing time, you can substitute a four-fold strap with rings (page 45).

PATTERN PIECES

- Front/Back bag body (pattern piece #1)
- Side panel (pattern piece #2)
- Facing (pattern piece #5)
- Lining (pattern piece #3)
- Lining side panel (pattern piece #4)
- Flap (pattern piece #21)
- Bag base (pattern piece #6)
- Bag base support (pattern piece #7)
- The strap, grab-handle, and zippered gusset pieces will be cut according to instructions.
- Choose any pocket pieces you want on the lining.

MATERIALS

- ½ yard decor-weight feature fabric for the outer bag*
- 1¾ yards medium-weight denim or decor-weight contrast fabric (You need the length for the strap and will have a lot of fabric left over for another project.)
- ⅛ yard plain, light fabric, color-matched to the contrast fabric (for the backs of the O-ring tabs)
- ⅔ yard quilting-weight fabric for the lining
- ⅓ yard heavyweight fast2fuse
- 1¾ yards medium woven fusible interfacing
- ½ yard light fusible fleece

(continued on page 160)

Materials, continued

- ⅛ yard medium-light woven fusible interfacing

- 1″ × 15″ nonwoven fusible interfacing (Vilene S320 or Pellon Craft-Fuse) for handles

- 8″ × 13″ pelmet interfacing (Vilene S520 or Pellon 520F Deco-Fuse) for bag base

- 2 O-rings 1″

- 2 rectangle rings 1½″

- 1 slide adjuster 1½″

- 2 twist locks

- 16″ zipper to match contrast fabric (for zippered gusset closure)

- 8″ zipper (for lining pocket)

- Template plastic

- 12″ × 20″ fusible webbing

- ¼″ fusible tape

- Fabric gluestick

- Strong, clear-drying craft glue (to attach fabric and metal)

- Scotch tape

- Fine-point fabric pencil

- Disappearing marker pen or Hera marker

* I used "Elka" by Pippiejoe.

ALTER THE PATTERN

1. Slash and close 3¼″ on horizontal slash line #1 on the bag body, side panel, lining, and lining side panel (see Slash and Close, page 27).

2. Slash and close ½″ on horizontal slash line #2 on each of the following pattern pieces: bag body, lining, bag base, and bag base support.

3. Slash and close ½″ on vertical slash line #2 on the following pattern pieces: facing, side panel, and lining side panel.

4. If using the divider pocket on the lining, slash and close 2½″ on horizontal slash line #1. If using the basic bag pocket (pattern piece #23), shorten it by 2″.

5. Label the new pattern pieces carefully so that you won't mix them up with the other bag patterns.

FUSE AND CUT THE FABRIC

NOTE:

To simplify the instructions for the straps and handle, the cutting instructions come as you need the individual pieces during the construction of the bag. You should cut the long strap pieces first, though, to make sure that you have enough fabric for them. For this bag, the shoulder strap is cut 4¼″ × 60″.

Prepare the Bag Body Pieces

1. Block fuse medium fusible woven interfacing and light fusible fleece to the wrong side of the feature fabric, and cut 2 bag body pieces. Mark all notches and dots on the wrong side of fabric.

2. On the wrong side of the bag body pieces, measure and draw a line 4½″ up from the base corner line. Measure and mark a line 2⅝″ in from each of the side edges. These are approximate placement marks for the twist-lock closures. (You will confirm the exact placement after adding the hole components of the lock to the flap.)

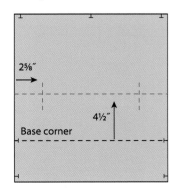

3. Block fuse medium-weight interfacing to the contrast fabric, and cut 2 side panel pieces.

4. Block fuse medium interfacing and cut 2 facing pieces in contrast fabric. Or if you prefer to cut and fuse separately, remove the seam allowances from the interfacing (trim 1″ from both length and width) before fusing.

5. Cut 1 bag base in contrast fabric. Cut 1 bag base support in pelmet interfacing (Vilene S520 or Pellon 520F Deco-Fuse) and 1 in template plastic.

6. Cut 2 each of the lining and lining side panel pieces in the lining fabric, and then cut the pockets that you'd like to make on the lining.

Prepare the Flap pieces

1. Block fuse medium woven interfacing and cut 1 flap (pattern piece #21) in feature fabric.

2. Cut 1 flap (pattern piece #21) in contrast fabric (don't block fuse) and 1 in medium woven interfacing.

3. Cut 1 fast2fuse piece 10″ × 11³⁄₈″. Take particular care to cut this straight and square, as it will determine the shape of the finished bag flap. The best way to do this is with a rotary cutter and quilting ruler.

4. Working on the ironing board, center the fast2fuse on the adhesive side of the interfacing piece, taking extra care to ensure that there is an even ½″ seam allowance around the edge of the interfacing.

5. Place the contrast fabric piece over the top of the fast2fuse, with the right side of fabric facing upward. Starting on the right side of fabric, and then turning to the interfacing side, fuse all layers together, aligning the edges of the fabric and interfacing to make an even seam

allowance around the fast2fuse. Be sure to fuse the seam allowance of the interfacing to the seam allowances of the flap piece.

THE FLAP

Make the Flap

1. Place the 2 flap pieces right sides together, and pin or bulldog clip them, with seam allowances aligned.

2. Beginning at the notch on the back edge, stitch toward the dot marking near the front edge of the flap, keeping the stitch line against the edge of the fast2fuse (without catching the fast2fuse in the seam).

NOTE:

Use a narrow zipper foot to stitch against the edge of the fast2fuse.

3. Pivot on the corner of the fast2fuse, and stitch to the other front corner. Pivot again, around the corner of the fast2fuse, and then stitch back to the other notch on the back edge of the flap. Even if the pattern-marking dot is sitting in from the edge of the fast2fuse, follow the line that the fast2fuse creates.

4. Remove the interfacing from the seam allowances of the flap, and clip the corners from the ends of the seam to 1¼″ down the sides. Press the seam allowances open.

5. Turn the flap to the right side and press it flat.

6. Topstitch around the 3 seamed sides of the flap, a scant ¼″ from the edge, and then topstitch another row, a scant ¼″ in from the first.

7. Apply quilt-basting spray between the outer and inner flap pieces to hold them together.

Insert the Twist-Lock Holes

1. On the underside (contrast fabric side) of the flap, measure and draw a Hera or disappearing marker line 1⅛″ from the bottom edge.

2. Measure and mark a ½″ vertical line, crossing the horizontal marker line, 1½″ in from each side edge of the flap.

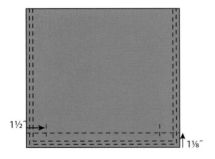

3. Center a back plate (the hole part) of the twist lock over each of the placement markings. Trace around the inside of the hole with fabric marker or pencil, marking the fabric where it will need to be cut away.

4. Use a point cutter, scalpel, utility knife, or hole punch to begin to cut the opening. Then, continuing to check against the lock components, carefully trim the fabric (little by little) with sharp scissors until no fabric can be seen in the hole area when the lock pieces are placed over the top.

5. Spread a thin layer of craft glue on the inside of a front plate of the twist lock, and then place it over the opening, on the right side of the flap. From the underside of the flap, press the fabric into the glue and to the inside of the front plate (so that no fabric will be seen in the opening.)

6. Spread a little craft glue on the inside of the back plate, and press it over the opening on the underside of the flap. Bend the prongs of the front plate over the back plate, and hammer them (lightly) into place.

7. Repeat Steps 4– 6 for the other twist-lock opening.

CONSTRUCT THE PADDED GRAB-HANDLE

Cutting straight lines and measuring accurately are vital here. The interfacing and the backing paper of the fusible webbing are used throughout the process as folding lines and as a means of keeping everything aligned squarely. It's therefore important to use a quilting ruler and rotary cutter (not scissors) and take care to measure and align everything accurately before fusing anything into place.

If you want to simplify the construction of this design, you can substitute four-fold straps with rings (page 45) for these handles.

Prepare the Upper Handle Piece

1. Cut 1 piece of interfacing (preferably Vilene S320 or Pellon Craft-Fuse) and 1 piece of paper-backed fusible webbing, each 1″ × 15″.

2. Measure and draw a line 2″ in from each short end of the webbing and interfacing.

3. Measure and mark ¼″ in from the sides on each short end of the webbing and the interfacing. Draw a diagonal line between the 2″ line on the long edges and the ¼″ mark on the short ends. Cut along the diagonal lines to taper the ends of the webbing. (To speed things up, you can layer the ends and cut several at a time.)

4. Place the interfacing on the wrong side of some scrap contrast fabric, aligning the length of the interfacing with the straight grain of the fabric and leaving enough space to cut a ½″ seam allowance around. Fuse the interfacing into place, and then fuse the fusible webbing over the top of the interfacing. Leave the backing paper on.

5. Use a rotary cutter and ruler to cut a ½″ seam allowance around the interfacing and fusible webbing.

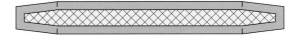

6. Using the backing paper of the fusible webbing as a fold line, turn and press the seam allowances over the top of the webbing and interfacing. Snip ¼″ into the seam allowances at the 2″ mark from each handle end. This will help the seam allowances to sit flat around the tapered end of the handle. Press the handle very flat to make the creases as sharp as possible.

7. On the tapered ends of each handle, trim the seam allowances from the end of the crease to 1″ along the long seam allowances, and then trim the rest of the seam allowance (at each of the tapered ends) so that the raw edges meet in the middle of the handle with no overlap.

8. Peel the backing paper off the handle and, placing it webbing-side down on an appliqué mat or baking paper, press to stick all of the seam allowances into place.

Prepare Inner Straps for the Handle and O-Ring Tabs

1. Cut 4 rectangles of paper-backed fusible webbing, 1″ × 4″.

2. On each piece, measure ¼″ in from each side on one of the short ends. Draw a line (or simply align a quilting ruler and cut with a rotary cutter) from this point to the opposite corner point on the same long side. This will taper the ends of the webbing.

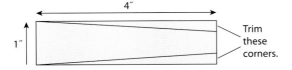

3. Press the webbing pieces onto the plain light fabric, following the straight grain of fabric (with the length of the webbing piece), allowing enough space around each piece to cut a ½″ seam allowance. Leave the backing paper on.

4. Cut each piece with a ½″ seam allowance along both of the long sides, and cut the short edges flush with the ends of the webbing.

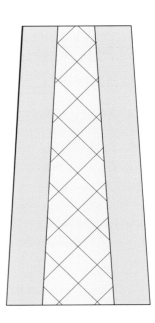

5. Use the backing paper of the webbing as a fold line to fold the seam allowances toward the webbing side of each piece. (Fig. A)

6. Clip the corners of the seam allowances from each of the creases to 1″ down the long, raw edges. (Fig. B)

7. Peel the backing paper off the inner straps and, placing them webbing-side down on an appliqué mat or baking paper, press to stick all of the seam allowances into place.

8. Keep 2 of these inner straps for the handle and put 2 aside to use on the O-ring tabs later.

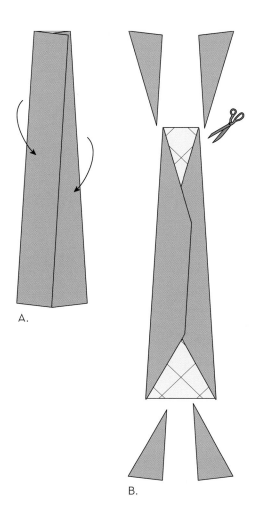

A.

B.

Prepare the Underside of the Handle

1. Cut a rectangle of contrast fabric 2″ × 10″.

2. Cut fast2fuse 1″ × 9″ and fuse it, centered, along the wrong side of the rectangle.

3. Using a Teflon mat or baking parchment to protect your iron, turn the long seam allowance edges over the fast2fuse, and press them flat and into place. Make sure that the crease is sharp and straight before proceeding—it's worth taking care here.

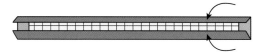

4. At each end, trim the seam allowances, using the corner rule (page 21), from the end of each crease to 1″ down the seam allowance. You may have to peel a little bit of the seam allowance away from the fast2fuse at the corners.

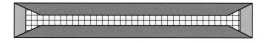

5. Fold each of the clipped points of the seam allowances inward (on a 45° angle), leaving a gap of ⅛″ between the end of the fast2fuse and the folded edge of the seam allowance. Use fabric gluestick or fusible tape to hold them in place.

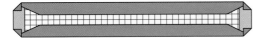

6. Fold the seam allowances (at both short ends) over the edge of the fast2fuse, and fuse or glue them into place, taking care to keep the corners square and straight.

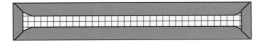

7. Cut 2 strips of fast2fuse (or a single strip of Peltex, which is thicker than fast2fuse) ½″ × 8″, and fuse them in the center, on the wrong side of the handle piece. Cover the fast2fuse with a Teflon mat or baking parchment, and press from both sides of the fabric.

Construct the Handle

1. On the wrong side of the upper handle piece, fuse or glue an inner strap piece to each end (wrong sides together), aligning the tapered end of each inner strap ½″ from the end of the handle piece.

2. On the right side of the upper handle, measure and draw a Hera or disappearing marker line 4″ in from each end.

3. On each side of the handle, topstitch ¹⁄₁₆″ from the edge, from each tapered end to the nearest marker line. Pivot and stitch a second row, ¼″ in from the first. This will hold the inner strap to the upper handle.

4. Push each tapered end through an O-ring, and fold the end to match both ends of the inner strap together, with the O-ring sitting in the fold. Pin, glue, or fuse the ends of the handle into place.

5. At both ends of each handle, topstitch (from the upper side) along the 4″ line, backstitching at each end of the stitch line. Pull all the excess threads through to the wrong side of fabric.

6. Cut a strip of fusible webbing 1″ × 9″ and fuse it, centered, on the wrong side of the upper handle, covering all the seam allowances. Remove the backing paper.

7. With wrong sides facing, center the underside of the handle on the upper handle. Iron with steam and pressure to fuse the two sides together. While it is still warm, use your fingers to pinch the edges together on either side of the fast2fuse strips in the middle. Add more fusible webbing as needed, and hold the handle pieces together with bulldog clips until they cool.

8. Across both ends of the upper handle piece, draw a Hera or disappearing marker line as a stitch guide for attaching the upper and lower handles together. The line needs to be a generous 1/16" in from each of the short ends of the underside piece, but drawn on the right side of the upper handle piece.

9. Topstitch (from the upper handle side) along the stitch guide on one end of the handle. Pivot and stitch 1/16" from the side edge to the other stitch guideline, and then continue to sew across and up the other side of the handle.

10. In a continuous line, topstitch 2 more rows along the length of each handle on either side of the fast2fuse padding in the middle.

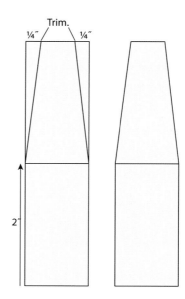

MAKE THE O-RING TABS

Prepare the O-Ring Tabs

1. Cut 2 strips of medium-weight fusible woven interfacing 1" × 4". Cut 2 strips of paper-backed fusible webbing 1" × 4".

2. On each of the interfacing and webbing strips, measure and draw a line 2" from one end.

3. On a short end on each strip, measure 1/4" from each side, and trim to taper the end in the same manner as the inner and upper handle ends.

4. Aligning the long edges of the strips with the straight grain of fabric, fuse the interfacing to the wrong side of a scrap of contrast fabric, leaving enough space to cut a 1/2" seam allowance around each piece.

5. Fuse the webbing over the interfacing (on the wrong side of fabric). Do not remove the backing paper.

6. Using a rotary cutter and ruler, measure and cut a 1/2" seam allowance around each of the interfacing pieces.

Construct the O-Ring Tabs

1. Use the edge of the backing paper and interfacing as a fold line to turn and press the seam allowances to the interfacing side. Snip 1/4" into the seam allowance at the 2" mark on each O-ring tab. This will allow the seam allowance to fold around the tapered end and sit flat. Press the turnings flat.

2. Trim the corners of the turnings from the end of each crease to 1″ down each long seam allowance edge, and then trim the seam allowances of the tapered end so that the raw edges meet in the middle (do not overlap).

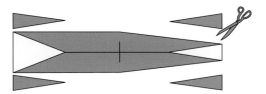

3. Remove the backing paper and, turning the webbing side on an appliqué mat or baking paper, press to stick the turnings securely into place.

4. On the square ends of each O-ring tab, fold the corners of the seam allowance in at a 45° angle, toward the wrong side of fabric, leaving ⅛″ clear between the short end of the interfacing and the folded corner fabric. Use fabric gluestick or fusible tape to hold the turnings in place.

5. Fold the seam allowance at the square end of each O-ring tab to the wrong side of fabric, using the edge of the interfacing as a fold line to keep the edge square and straight. Place the webbing side of the handle on an appliqué mat or baking paper, and then press to fuse the turning into place.

6. Place the inner strap prepared earlier (page 165) from light fabric and O-ring tab wrong sides together, aligning the raw edges at the tapered end. Glue or fuse the inner straps in place, covering the turnings of the O-ring tab. If any raw (or turned) ends of the inner strap overhang the outer O-ring tab, fold and stick them inward.

7. On the right side of each O-ring tab, measure and draw a line (with a Hera or disappearing marker) 1½″ from the square end. Draw a second line 1¼″ in from the same end.

8. On each O-ring tab, between the tapered end and the 1½″ mark, topstitch 1/16″ in from each folded edge. Pivot and turn to stitch a second row on each edge, ¼″ in from the first.

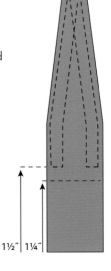

1½″ | 1¼″

Attach the O-Ring Tabs to the Handles

1. With the right side of fabric facing outward, thread the tapered end of each O-ring tab through an O-ring at each end of the handle. Match the tapered end of each tab to the raw edge of the turning at the other (square) end of the tab. Pin, glue, or fuse the tapered end in place, keeping any adhesives within 1½″ of the square end.

2. From the right side of fabric, topstitch across each of the 1¼″ marker lines, backstitching neatly at both ends.

3. Cut 2 pieces of fusible webbing 1″ × 1½″, and fuse each to the square end of an O-ring tab.

Attach the Handle to the Flap

1. On the right side of the flap, measure and draw a Hera or disappearing marker line 1″ in from the back (raw) edge. Measure in 1″ from each of the side edges, and draw a line at this point, from the back edge of the flap to the horizontal line, on both sides of the flap.

2. Matching the square end of each tab to the vertical marker lines, with one side edge of each tab aligned with the horizontal line, place both the O-ring tabs on the flap piece. Use a combination of heat, steam, and pressure to press and fuse the tabs into place. If the fabric is too thick and won't fuse properly, use pins.

3. Topstitch the tabs to the flap 1/16″ from the edge, from the 1½″ marker line to the bottom of the tab, across the square end, and back to the 2″ line. Pivot and turn to stitch a second row ¼″ in from the first, around the square end of the tab, and then back across the 1½″ marker line. Backstitch neatly and pull all the threads through to the wrong side of fabric.

ATTACH THE TWIST LOCK TO THE BAG BODY

Twist locks vary in design and require slightly different methods to insert. It is important to reinforce the fabric around the metal components. These instructions are for a basic prong-based twist lock. You can adapt them to work with the twist locks that are available to you.

1. On the wrong side of the front bag body piece, place the twist-lock openings on the front of the finished flap over the approximate twist-lock placement marks. Center the flap carefully along the horizontal line, and mark the center point of each hole with a dot or cross.

2. Place the twist part of each lock over a placement marking, with the prongs spaced evenly on either side of the dot. Mark the fabric to show where the prongs sit.

3. Using small scissors, a point cutter, or a small scalpel, cut ¼" slits on the fabric in the prong-placement marks.

4. From your scraps of fast2fuse (or use Timtex or Peltex), cut 2 rectangles 1½" × 2". From your template plastic scraps, cut 2 rectangles 1" × 1½". Trim the sharp corners off the template plastic rectangles to make them a little rounder. These are to reinforce the fabric around the lock.

5. Mark the prong-placement marks in the center of each reinforcement piece (template plastic and fast2fuse/Peltex/Timtex), and slit each mark with a point cutter or scalpel.

6. From the right side of fabric, push the twist-lock prongs through the slits in the fabric. On the wrong side of fabric, push a rectangle of fast2fuse/Peltex/Timtex over the prongs of each twist lock, and then push a piece of template plastic over that. Push the back plate of the twist lock over the template plastic, and bend the prongs firmly inward (a gentle tap with a hammer can be good).

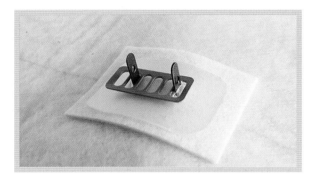

7. Cut 2 more rectangles of fast2fuse, Peltex, or Timtex 2″ × 3″. If using double-sided fusible Peltex or fast2fuse, cover and fuse one side with fabric or interfacing. These are to cover the backs of the twist locks, to protect the lining fabric.

8. Center each of the rectangles over the back of a twist lock (on the wrong side of fabric), and pin them in place from the right side of fabric.

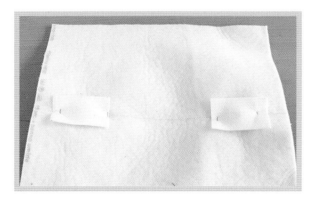

9. Use a Hera or disappearing marker to draw a rectangle shape around each of the twist locks, following the shape of the fast2fuse, Peltex, or Timtex rectangle on the inside.

10. Stitch around each twist lock, following the marker line, and then remove the marker line.

MAKE THE BAG BASE

1. On the pelmet interfacing, mark the purse feet positions 1″ from the long edges of the base, 1½″ in from each of the short ends, and in the center of the long horizontal placement lines.

2. Follow the directions in Structured External Base with Purse Feet (page 55).

CONSTRUCT THE BAG BODY

Follow the instructions for constructing the basic bag (page 66). As you sew each side seam, remove fleece and interfacing from the side seams, clip the seam allowances using the corner rule (page 21), and press the side seam allowances open.

MAKE THE SHOULDER STRAP

Construct the O-Ring Loops

1. Cut 2 rectangles of feature fabric 3″ × 4¼″, with the straight grain running parallel to the 3″ edge.

2. Cut 2 fusible woven interfacing pieces 2½″ × 3″. Center each piece of interfacing horizontally along the 3″ fabric strips.

3. Fold each rectangle to match the 3″ sides (right sides of fabric together), and follow the instructions (page 49) to make bagged-out O-ring loops.

4. Fold each O-ring loop (right side facing out) through a rectangle bag ring, and pin the raw ends of the strap together.

5. Draw a Hera or disappearing marker line across the strap, ¾″ from the folded edge (with the ring in it).

6. Stitch the strap ends together ¹⁄₁₆″ from a side edge; then pivot and stitch across the marker line and back down the other edge of the strap (see note on page 50).

Construct the Shoulder Strap

1. Cut a strap 4¼″ × 60″ from the contrast fabric.

2. Cut interfacing 2″ × 58″ and fuse it, centered, on the wrong side of the strap fabric.

3. Follow the instructions for making a bagged-out strap with rings at both ends (page 46).

4. Follow the instructions for making an adjustable strap (page 50) to attach the slide adjuster and to connect the strap to the rings.

Attach the Shoulder Strap

1. Place an O-ring tab on each of the side panels, right sides of fabric together and aligning the raw edges of the loops with the top edge of the bag. Check that there are no twists in the strap and that it is sitting right side down on the right side of the bag fabric.

2. Stitch the O-ring tabs to the seam allowances at the top edge of the side panels.

ATTACH THE FLAP

Follow the instructions (page 45) to attach the flap to the bag body, taking care to move the handle out of the way as you sew.

MAKE AND ATTACH THE FACING

1. Follow the instructions in Basic Bag (page 71) to make and attach the facing to the top edge of the bag. It may be a little awkward to sew past the flap and grab-handle, so use as many pins or bulldog clips as you need, and experiment until you find the presser foot that performs the task most effectively.

2. Remove the interfacing from the seam allowances of the bag (and facing if necessary), and then understitch the facing (page 72).

3. Turn the facing to the inside of the bag, and press it into place; then topstitch ⅜″ from the edge around the top of the bag. Change the thread color to match the 2 different fabrics as you topstitch.

MAKE THE ZIPPERED CLOSURE

1. Cut 2 interfacing pieces 3″ × 12″, and follow the zippered gusset instructions (page 59) to make the zipper closure for the top of the bag.

2. Cut a rectangle of interfacing (or fast2fuse) 1½″ × 3″, and make a tab for the end of the zipper (page 63).

MAKE THE LINING

1. Follow the instructions (pages 28–36) to add the pockets of your choice to the lining pieces. If using the compartment pocket, move the placement so that the bottom edge sits above the base corner point of the lining.

2. Follow the instructions in Basic Bag (page 74) to construct the lining.

ATTACH THE LINING

Follow the instructions (page 75) to attach the lining to the facing.

FINISH THE BAG

1. Anchor the lining to the base seams of the side panels (page 76).

2. Slipstitch (ladder stitch) to close the gap in the base seam of the lining.

THE TORONTO
CONVERTIBLE TOTE-BACKPACK

FINISHED BAG: 12½" × 15" × 5½"

This bag has convertible straps that can be moved and adjusted to make a backpack or a long- or short-strapped shoulder bag. It has a drawstring and a magnetic closure, which allows the shape of the bag to convert from square to triangular. It's adaptable, comfortable, and the sort of bag you'll carry everywhere with you. This project includes a lot of functional design details. For instance, a gusseted, zipped pocket on the front of the bag is fully lined and bound, and there is an exposed zipper on the back of the bag (a secure exterior pocket if the bag is worn as a backpack).

Take your time with this project, and work carefully through the instructions. They will guide you through lots of clever ways to achieve a highly professional finish and a very functional bag.

PATTERN PIECES

- Front/Back bag body (pattern piece #1)
- Side panel (pattern piece #2)
- Lining (pattern piece #3)
- Lining side panel (pattern piece #4)
- Facing (pattern piece #5)
- Bag base (pattern piece #6)
- Bag base support (pattern piece #7)
- Zipper pocket 2 facing (pattern piece #11)
- Toronto pocket (pattern piece #19)
- Toronto flap (pattern piece #20)
- Basic bag pocket (pattern piece #23)
- Choose any pocket pieces you want to include on the lining. Because this bag has so much detail on the outside, you may wish to keep the lining pockets very simple.

MATERIALS

- 1¼ yards decor-weight fabric for outer bag (main fabric)*
- 1½ yards quilting-weight contrast fabric for straps and pocket
- 2 yards quilting-weight fabric for lining**
- 2¾ yards light woven interfacing
- 7" × 13" heavyweight fast2fuse, Timtex, or Peltex for base support

(continued on page 176)

Materials, continued

- 3" × 12" nonwoven fusible interfacing (Vilene S320 or Pellon Craft-Fuse) for exposed zipper pocket lining
- 2" × 8" fusible webbing
- 1 zipper 8" to match the main or contrast fabric (for external exposed zipper pocket)
- 1 nylon zipper 16"–18" to match contrast fabric (for gusseted zipper pocket)
- 1 zipper 8" to match the lining fabric (for zipper pocket on the lining)
- 40" × ¼" or ⅜" cord
- 1 or 2 heavy 1" rings
- 1 cord pull
- 5 D-rings 1"

- 6 swivel hooks ¾" or 1"
- 3 slide adjusters 1"
- ¼" fusible tape
- Fabric gluestick
- Scotch tape
- Fine-point fabric pencil
- Disappearing marker pen or Hera marker
- Matching threads for all fabrics
- Teflon appliqué mat or baking parchment

* I used "Waratah Blossoms" by Veritas Designs for the outer bag.

**I used fabric by Saffron Craig for the lining.

ALTER THE PATTERN

> **NOTE:**
>
> *If you have made Galapagos Boho (page 124), you can use the same pattern pieces.*

1. Slash and close 1" on each horizontal slash line #2 on each of the following pattern pieces: bag body, lining, bag base, and bag base support (see Slash and Close, page 27).

2. Slash and close 1" on each vertical slash line #2 on the following pattern pieces: facing, side panel, and lining side panel.

3. Label the new pattern pieces carefully, so that you won't mix them up with the other bag patterns.

4. Trace a copy of the Toronto pocket pattern without a seam allowance to use as a template to trace the pocket placement onto the bag body.

5. Choose the pocket pieces you would like to use for the lining of the bag, and gather the pattern pieces.

FUSE AND CUT THE FABRIC

NOTE:

The cutting instructions for some bag components are presented with the instructions. When the bag has many different pieces (all looking remarkably similar in rectangular shape), it is often less confusing to cut as you go, rather than laying out and cutting each fabric as a whole. You should cut the long strap pieces first, though, to make sure that you have enough fabric for them. For this bag, the 3 shoulder straps are cut 4" × 33" each.

1. Block fuse lightweight interfacing to the main fabric, and cut 2 each of the bag body, side panel, and facing pieces.

2. Cut the bag base from the main fabric, and cut the bag base support in heavyweight fast2fuse, Timtex, or Peltex.

3. For the exposed zipper on the back of the bag, cut a zipper pocket 2 facing piece from the main fabric. Cut interfacing using the same pattern piece, but do not fuse them together yet.

4. Block fuse interfacing to both main and contrast fabrics, and cut 1 Toronto flap in each fabric. In the contrast fabric, also cut a 1³⁄₈" × 24" strip of wide bias tape, and run it through a ³⁄₄" bias tape maker to make bias binding (or carefully fold and press as for a four-fold strap, page 45).

5. For the drawstring casings, cut 2 rectangles of contrast fabric 3" × 37".

6. Cut a pocket lining for the exposed zipper on the back of the bag in lining or contrast fabric, using the basic bag pocket.

7. In lining fabric, cut 2 each of the lining and lining side panel pieces, and then cut the pockets that you'd like to make on the bag lining.

Prepare the Straps

1. Cut 3 shoulder straps 4" × 33" from the contrast fabric. Cut 3 light interfacing strips 2" × 31" and fuse them, centered, along the wrong side of each of the straps.

2. For the D-ring tabs, cut a strap 4" × 13" in contrast fabric. Cut a piece of light interfacing 2" × 13", and fuse it along the center of the strap, on the wrong side of fabric.

3. For the flap detail, cut a strap 4" × 9½" in contrast fabric. Do not fuse interfacing to this strap.

Prepare the Front Pocket

1. Block fuse interfacing and cut 1 Toronto pocket in both the contrast and lining fabrics. Use quilt-basting spray to hold the 2 pieces together, with right sides of fabric facing out. Cut tiny snips (a scant ⅛") at the notch marks on the pattern. Mark the dot points at the bottom corners of the pocket on the right side of the lining.

2. For the upper (zipper) pocket gussets, cut 1 strip 1³⁄₈" × 17⁵⁄₈" and 1 strip 1⅛" × 17⁵⁄₈" in contrast fabric, with the straight grain of fabric running along the length of the strips. Label the back of the wider of these 2 strips "A" and the narrower one "B." We'll refer to these as "Gusset A" and "Gusset B."

3. Cut 2 strips of interfacing ⁵⁄₈" × 16⁵⁄₈".

4. Fuse an interfacing strip to the wrong side of Gusset A, centered between the short ends and ½" away from one of the long edges (making it ¼" in from the other long edge). Fuse the other interfacing strip to the wrong side of Gusset B, centered between the short ends and ¼" in from each of the long edges.

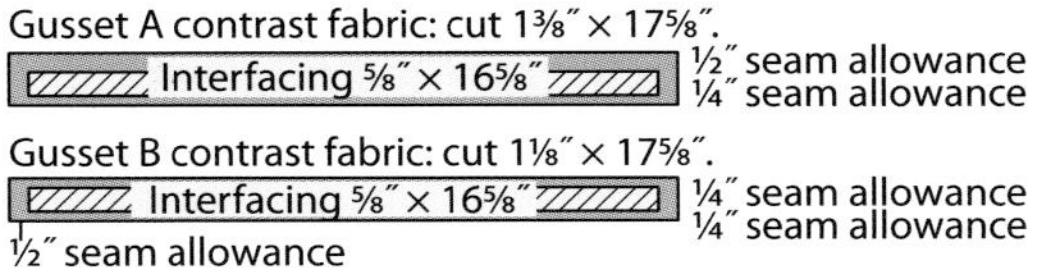

Gusset A contrast fabric: cut 1⅜" × 17⅝".

////	Interfacing ⅝" × 16⅝"	////

½" seam allowance
¼" seam allowance

Gusset B contrast fabric: cut 1⅛" × 17⅝".

////	Interfacing ⅝" × 16⅝"	////

¼" seam allowance
¼" seam allowance
½" seam allowance

5. To make lining for the upper (zipper) pocket gussets, cut 2 strips 1⅛" × 17½" in lining fabric, with the straight grain of fabric running along the length. Label these strips "C" and "D."

6. For the lower pocket gusset, cut 1 rectangle 2¼" × 18⅞" in contrast fabric, with the straight grain of fabric running along the length.

7. Cut 1 interfacing strip 1½" × 17⅞". Fuse the interfacing to the back of the gusset piece, ½" in from one long edge and ¼" from the other, and centered between the 2 short ends. Label this piece "E."

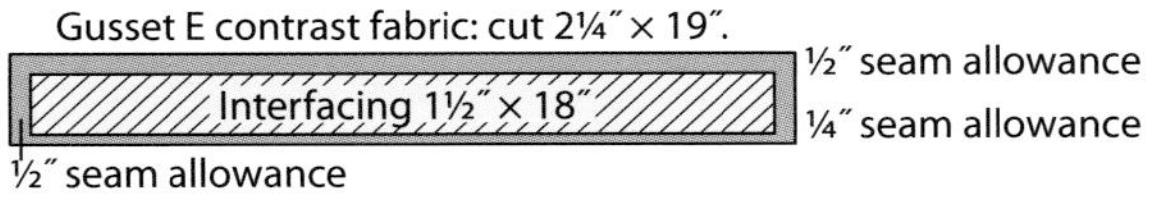

Gusset E contrast fabric: cut 2¼" × 19".

/////	Interfacing 1½" × 18"

½" seam allowance
¼" seam allowance
½" seam allowance

8. For the lower pocket gusset lining, cut 1 rectangle 2" × 18⅞", with the straight grain of fabric running along the length. Measure and draw a disappearing marker line (on the right side of fabric) across the width of this piece, 4¹⁄₁₆" from each short end. Label this piece "F."

9. Cut a 1⅜" × 36" bias strip in lining fabric, or join several shorter lengths, and run it through a ¾" bias tape maker to make bias binding (or fold and press carefully as for a four-fold strap, page 45).

MAKE THE GUSSETED ZIPPER POCKET

Insert the Zipper

1. Place Gusset A horizontally in front of you, right side of fabric facing up and with the ¼" seam allowance (that's the littler bit without interfacing) to the top. Place the 16" or 18" zipper right side down on the right side of fabric, with the opening end of the zipper toward the right-hand side.

2. Match the edge of the zipper tape to the edge of the narrow seam allowance. If using a 16" zipper, check that the metal stoppers at each end of the zipper are within the ½" seam allowance at each of the short ends of the gusset (an 18" zipper will run off the gusset). With the zipper tape in this position, stitch ¼" from the edge, to attach it along the full length of the gusset.

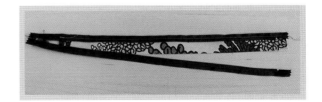

3. Place one of the lining fabric pieces (Gusset C) over the top of the zipper and Gusset A, with right sides of fabric facing (and the zipper sandwiched between). Align the long edge of the lining piece with the edge of the zipper tape, and stitch it into place, following the line of stitching on Gusset A.

4. Fold Gusset C to the right side, and under-stitch (page 72) it to hold it back from the zipper.

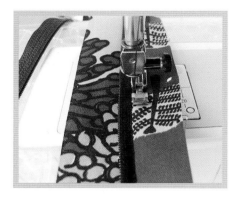

5. Fold and press the gusset and lining so that they sit with wrong sides together, with Gusset A extending past the outer edge of its lining by ¼". Use fabric gluestick, quilt-basting spray, or fusible tape to hold the 2 pieces together in this position.

6. Match Gusset B to the right side of the zipper, with the right sides of Gussets A and B together. Align the ¼" seam allowance edge of Gusset B to the edge of the zipper tape, and stitch the full length of the gusset piece, ¼" from the edge.

7. Match Gusset D (the other lining piece) to the back of the zipper, with right sides of fabric

facing. Stitch it into place, ¼" in from the edge of the zipper tape (following the line of stitching on Gusset B).

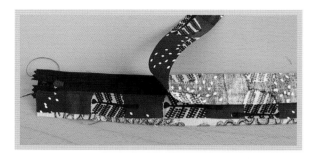

8. Understitch Gusset D (the lining) as in Step 4, and then press and stick the gusset pieces wrong sides together (see Step 5).

9. Topstitch the full length of the zipper gusset, ¹⁄₁₆" from the seam edge, on both sides of the zipper.

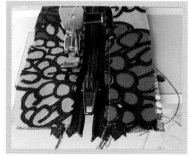

10. Whipstitch the open ends of the zipper together (page 34). If using an 18" zipper, zigzag over the other end of the zipper chain, and trim off the excess zipper.

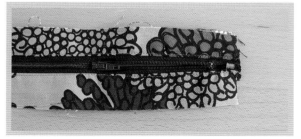

Attach the Lower Pocket Gusset

1. Place Gusset E over the outer side of the (zippered) upper gusset, with right sides of fabrics together and the ½" seam allowance matched to the overhanging seam allowance of Gusset A. Pin.

NOTE:

If the upper and lower gusset pieces are different widths once the zipper is inserted, trim excess from the ¼" seam allowance side (not the ½" side).

2. Match Gusset F (the lining) to the lining side of the zipped gusset, with right sides of fabric together and aligning all the outer edges of Gussets C and D. The outer edge of Gussets A and E should overhang Gusset F by ¼". Match the short ends of Gusset F to the short ends of the other gusset pieces. Reposition the pins to hold all the layers, and sew the seam with a ½" seam allowance.

3. Clip the corners of the seam allowances from each end of the short seams to a point in the middle.

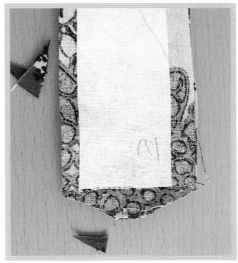

4. Turn Gussets E and F to the right side of fabric (wrong sides together), and press the seams flat. Carefully align the ¼" seam allowances, and check that the other edge of Gusset E overhangs Gusset F by ¼". Use fabric gluestick, quilt-basting spray, or fusible web to stick them in this position.

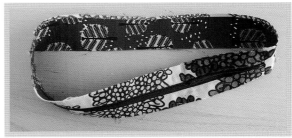

5. Topstitch both seams that join the upper and lower gusset pieces, on the lower gusset side, 1/16" from the seam.

6. Fold the overhanging 1/4" seam allowance of Gussets A and B over to the lining side, using the edge of the lining as a fold line, and press a crease. This can be awkward, so take care not to burn your fingers.

7. Fuse 1/4" fusible tape on the lining side, covering the 1/4" turning, around the pocket piece edge.

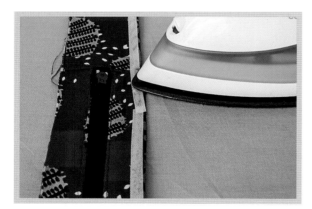

Attach the Front of the Pocket

1. Fold the finished gusset to match the 2 short seams together, folding the upper and lower gussets in half, crosswise. This will show you where the top and bottom center points are. Mark them with a marker or tiny snips on the lining side of the gusset.

2. With the right sides of the outer (contrast) fabrics together, match the seams of the gusset pieces to the notches on the pocket. Pin these into place.

3. Working with the pocket piece to the top, align the dot on the bottom-right corner of the lining with the 4" marker line on the gusset lining. Place a pin horizontally, following the line of the 4" marker line, to hold it to the pocket in this position.

4. Beginning 1" above one of the side notches, stitch the pocket to the gusset with a 1/4" seam allowance, toward the bottom corner. As you near the corner, slow down so that you can stop right at the dot marking.

5. Reverse stitch from the dot, about 1″ back along the seam. Use sharp scissors to snip through the seam allowance of the gusset to the stitch line. Take care not to snip any stitches.

6. Turn the unattached part of the gusset to align its edge with the bottom edge of the pocket. The snip in the seam allowance will allow it to turn the corner sharply.

7. Sew back along the seamline to the corner point, and lower the needle into the last stitch. Lift the presser foot and pivot to continue sewing the base of the pocket to the gusset. The marker point at the center will help to keep the fabric alignment on track.

8. Match the next 4″ marker line on the lining to the dot marking on the next corner. Sew to the corner, and repeat the reverse-snip-pivot method (Steps 2–6) to sew the gusset around the corner.

9. Keep sewing around the pocket piece, ¼″ from the edge, gently easing the curve of the pocket onto the gusset until you reach the starting point again, pinning as necessary. The center notches

at the top of the pocket will help you keep the pocket and gusset aligned.

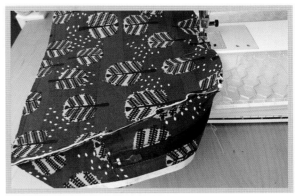

Bind the Pocket Seam

1. Place the bias binding (made from lining fabric) along the bottom edge of the pocket with right sides of fabric together. Align the folded edge of the bias tape with the seamline.

2. Open the folded edge of the binding and, leaving ¾″ from the end of the binding free, begin to stitch along the fold line to attach it to the pocket seam. Use the snip-and-pivot method (see Attach the Front of the Pocket, Steps 2–6) to turn the binding around the bottom corners, and use the flexibility of the bias grain to attach the binding around the curved edges.

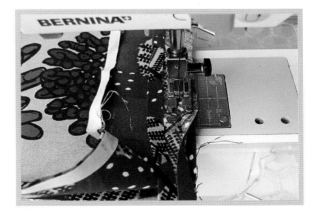

3. As you near the beginning of the binding, fold the loose end inward (toward the wrong side of the binding). Continue to align and sew the binding over the seamline (and the folded end of the binding) until the overlap is ¾" over the folded beginning of the binding. Trim off the excess.

4. Fold and press the binding over the raw edges to the other side of the seam. Trim the seam allowance back as necessary, to allow the folded edge of the binding to sit ¹⁄₁₆" over the seamline.

5. Use a tailor's awl to hold the binding ¹⁄₁₆" over the seamline, and miter the bottom corners as you topstitch the binding into place.

NOTES:

- *Don't panic if your stitching isn't super-neat; nobody will ever inspect it inside the pocket.*

- *Don't be tempted to handstitch the binding into place; the structure in the pocket seam will be lost if you do that.*

Attach the Pocket

1. Place a ruler across the front bag body pieces 4¼" above the bottom edge, and draw a Hera or disappearing marker line all the way across, on the right side of fabric.

2. Center the bottom edge of the pocket template (without seam allowances) on the marker line, and trace around it with a fine-point fabric pencil or disappearing marker. This is the pocket placement mark.

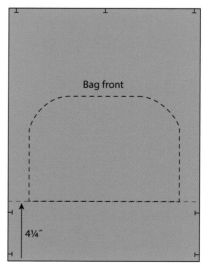

3. Remove the backing paper from the fusible tape, and place the pocket on the right side of a bag body piece, aligning the bottom edge with the marker line. Position the pocket over the placement mark, and press (little by little) to fuse it to the bag body; use pins as necessary to hold the pocket securely.

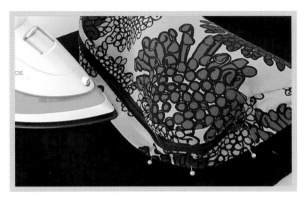

4. Beginning on the bottom edge of the pocket, topstitch 1/16" from the edge all the way around the pocket.

5. Stitch another row of top stitching 1/8" in from the first, but stitch out to the corner points at the bottom of the pocket to avoid puckers.

Make the Exposed Zipper on the Back of the Bag

1. Follow the instructions in Exposed Zipper Pocket (page 36) to prepare and fuse the interfacing to the zipper pocket 2 facing piece that is cut in the main fabric.

2. On the back bag body piece, on the right side of fabric, measure and mark a Hera or disappearing marker line 2½" in from the left-hand-side edge. Measure and mark the line 2½" down from the top edge of the bag.

3. Place the pocket facing piece on the back bag body piece, right side down on the right side of fabric. Match the top outer corner of the pocket facing with the point where the 2 lines intersect, and align the long edge with the vertical line. (The zipper will sit vertically on the back of the bag.)

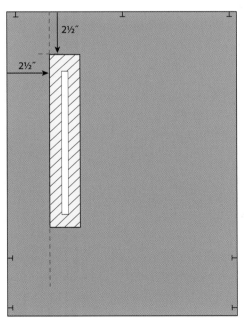

4. Follow the instructions in Exposed Zipper Pocket (page 36) to construct a pocket, using the pocket piece cut in contrast fabric.

D-Ring Tabs

1. Use the 4″ × 13″ strap to make a four-fold strap (page 45). Topstitch as usual.

2. Cut the strap into 5 lengths 2½″ (trim off excess), and fold each of these through a 1″ D-ring.

3. Match the 2 raw ends of each tab, and stitch them together, ¹⁄₁₆″ from both side edges and across the strap, as close to the base of the D-ring as possible.

TIP:

Use a narrow zipper foot so that you can stitch close to the bottom of the D-ring.

4. On the right side of the back bag body piece, measure 1½″ above each of the base corner notches, and mark the seam allowance with a small nick or marker line. These are the D-ring placement marks.

5. Working on the right side of the bag body fabric, match the raw ends of a D-ring tab to each side edge of the bag piece, centered over the D-ring placement marks. Stitch ¼″ from the edge of the fabric to hold the D-ring tabs in this position.

6. Still working on the right side of fabric, match a D-ring tab to the center notch on the top edge of the back bag body piece, aligning the raw edges of the tabs with the raw edge of the top seam allowance. Stitch ¼″ from the edge of the fabric to hold the tab in this position.

7. Center a D-ring tab over the center notch on the top edge (on the right side of fabric) of each of the side panel pieces. Align the raw edges of the

tab with the seam allowance edge, and stitch them together ¼″ from the edge of fabric.

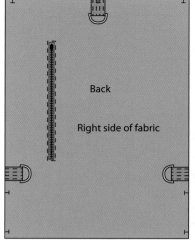
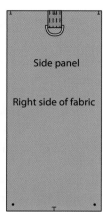

Back — Right side of fabric

Side panel — Right side of fabric

MAKE THE BAG BASE

Follow the directions (page 53) for the external textile base.

CONSTRUCT THE BAG BODY

Follow the instructions for the basic bag (page 66) to construct the bag. As you sew each side seam, remove interfacing from the side seams, clip the seam allowances using the corner rule (page 21), and press the side seam allowances open.

THE FLAP

Make the Flap Detail Strap

1. Using the 4″ × 9½″ strap, follow the instructions to fold and press a four-fold strap (page 45). Use quilt-basting spray or fusible webbing to hold the strap together, ready for top stitching.

2. Topstitch 2 rows along the middle of the strap, ³⁄₈″ from each long side edge.

3. Using a ruler and Hera (or disappearing) marker, draw a line across the strap, 3½″ from one of the short ends.

4. Between the end of the strap and the 3½″ marker line, topstitch ¹⁄₁₆″ in from one of the side edges, across the marker line, and then ¹⁄₁₆″ down the other side edge.

5. Fold the top-stitched end of the strap 2″ from the end, and thread a heavy bag ring (or 2) over the fold.

6. Cut and fuse a 1″ × 6″ strip of fusible webbing to the back of the strap, from the (newly top-stitched) 3½″ mark to the end of the strap. Remove the backing paper.

7. On the right side of the main fabric flap piece, center the strap and align the raw edge of the strap with the back edge of the flap. Fuse the strap into place.

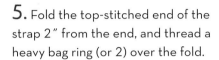

TIP:

After you have fused the strap into place, and while the fusible adhesive is still warm, use a tailor's awl to poke in the raw edges of the folded strap end. Press the strap again to make the ends stay put.

8. Using a ruler and Hera (or disappearing) marker, draw a line across the strap, 1¼″ from the folded edge (near the O-ring).

9. Beginning at the back edge, topstitch the strap to the flap piece, ¹⁄₁₆″ from one side edge, across the new marker line, and then back along the other side, ¹⁄₁₆″ from the edge.

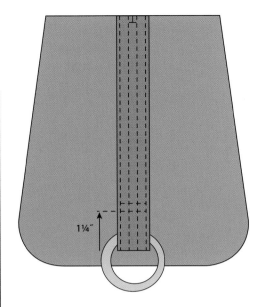

Construct the Flap

1. Place the outer and underside flap pieces wrong sides together. Use quilt-basting spray (or old-fashioned hand- or machine-basting stitches) to hold the 2 pieces together, in complete alignment.

2. Beginning at the back edge of the flap, with the underside of the flap facing upward, unfold one side of the bias binding strip from contrast fabric, and align its raw edge to the edge of the flap. Stitch the binding around the sides and front of the flap, following the (opened) fold line in the binding. Use the stretch in the bias grain of the tape to ease the binding around the curved edge of the flap. Do not sew binding across the straight back edge of the flap.

3. Fold the binding over to the outer side of the flap, and check to see if it covers the line of stitching from the other side of the binding (it probably won't). Trim off just enough of the outer edge of the flap to allow the binding to overlap the stitching on the right side of the outer piece by ¹⁄₁₆″.

4. Fold and press the binding into place on the right side of the outer flap, taking care to align the folded edge of the binding ¹⁄₁₆″ over the stitch line, around the front and sides of the flap.

TIP:

Use a fabric gluestick to help hold the binding into place.

5. Topstitch the binding to the right side of the outer flap piece, holding the folded edge in place with a tailor's awl just in front of the presser foot as you sew.

Attach the Flap

1. Place the flap on the back bag body piece, right sides of fabric together, and match the center-back notches together.

2. Align the raw edges of the seam allowances, and stitch the flap into place, ³⁄₈″ from the edge of the seam allowance.

MAKE THE CASING

1. Match the 2 casing pieces (contrast fabric 3″ × 37″) right sides together, and sew across each of the short ends with a ¹⁄₂″ seam allowance.

2. Clip the corners of the seam allowance from each end of each seam to 1¹⁄₄″ down the edge of the seam allowance, and press the seam open.

3. Turn the casing pieces right side out, and press them wrong sides together, aligning the long, raw edges and folding sharply on each of the seamlines.

4. Topstitch the seamed short ends of the casing, ¹⁄₁₆″ from the edge, and then stitch another row ¹⁄₄″ in from the first row.

5. Fold the casing in half lengthwise (matching the long, raw edges together), and press a crease along the fold line. Stitch all the layers together, ¹⁄₄″ in from the raw edges.

Fold.

6. Fold the casing in half crosswise (matching the 2 short ends together), and snip a small notch to mark the center point on the seam allowance. Now fold each short end to the center point, and snip a notch on the seam allowance to mark each ¹⁄₄″ point.

7. Working on the right side of the bag body, match a short end of the casing to the center-front notch on the top edge of the bag body. Align the raw edges of the seam allowances, and pin the casing into place. Continue to pin the casing around the top edge of the bag, matching the quarter-point notches to the center notches on the side panels and the center notch to the center-back notch on the back of the bag (and flap). Align the other short end of the casing, flush with the first, at the center-front.

8. Stitch the casing to the top edge of the bag, ³⁄₈" in from the raw edges, and then remove the interfacing from the seam allowances of the bag body.

MAKE AND ATTACH THE FACING

Follow the instructions in Basic Bag (page 71) to make and attach the facing to the top edge of the bag.

INSERT THE MAGNETIC SNAP

Follow the instructions (page 58) to insert a magnetic snap in the facing.

MAKE THE LINING

1. Follow the instructions (pages 28–36) to add the pockets of your choice to the lining pieces.

2. Follow the instructions in Basic Bag (page 74) to construct the lining.

ATTACH THE LINING

Follow the instructions (page 76) to attach the lining to the facing.

ADJUSTABLE, CONVERTIBLE SHOULDER STRAPS

1. Using the 3 shoulder strap (4″ × 33″) pieces, follow the instructions to make four-fold straps with a ring at both ends (page 45).

2. Follow the instructions to make an adjustable strap (page 50) with each of the shoulder straps, but use swivel hooks instead of O-rings at each end of the strap.

FINISH THE BAG

1. Anchor the lining to the base seams of the side panels (page 75).

2. Slipstitch (ladder stitch) to close the gap in the base seam of the lining.

3. Attach a strap between the 2 side panel D-rings, and shorten it to a comfortable grab-handle or shoulder-strap length. Attach the other 2 straps between the center-back D-ring and each of the 2 D-rings near the base corner.

4. Thread cord through the casing, and attach a cord pull. You can add cord ends to the cord, or simply tie secure knots in each end.